INTO THE FAERIE HILL

H. S. NORUP is the award-winning author of *The Hungry Ghost* and *The Missing Barbegazi*—a *Sunday Times* Book of the Year in 2018. She grew up in Denmark, where she devoured fairy tales and escaped into books. After living in six different countries, she now resides in Switzerland and writes stories inspired by her travels, set in the borderlands between the real and imaginary worlds. When she's not writing or reading, she spends her time outdoors either skiing, hiking, swimming or taking photos.

ALSO BY H.S. NORUP

The Missing Barbegazi
The Hungry Ghost
The Changeling Child

PUSHKIN CHILDREN'S

INTO THE FAERIE HILL

H.S. NORUP

Pushkin Press
Somerset House, Strand
London WC2R 1LA

Copyright © 2023 H.S. Norup

Into the Faerie Hill was first published by Pushkin Press in 2023

ISBN 13: 978-1-78269-386-4

All rights reserved. No part of this publication may be reproduced, stored in a retrieval system or transmitted in any form or by any means, electronic, mechanical, photocopying, recording or otherwise, without prior permission in writing from Pushkin Press

A CIP catalogue record for this title is available from the British Library

The authorised representative in the EEA is
eucomply OÜ, Pärnu mnt. 139b-14, 11317, Tallinn, Estonia,
hello@eucompliancepartner.com, +33757690241

Designed and typeset by Tetragon, London
Printed and bound in the United Kingdom by Clays Ltd, Elcograf S.p.A.

Pushkin Press is committed to a sustainable future for our business, our readers and our planet. This book is made from paper from forests that support responsible forestry.

www.pushkinpress.com

3 5 7 9 8 6 4 2

*For Far—my dad—and all fathers
who raise children on their own*

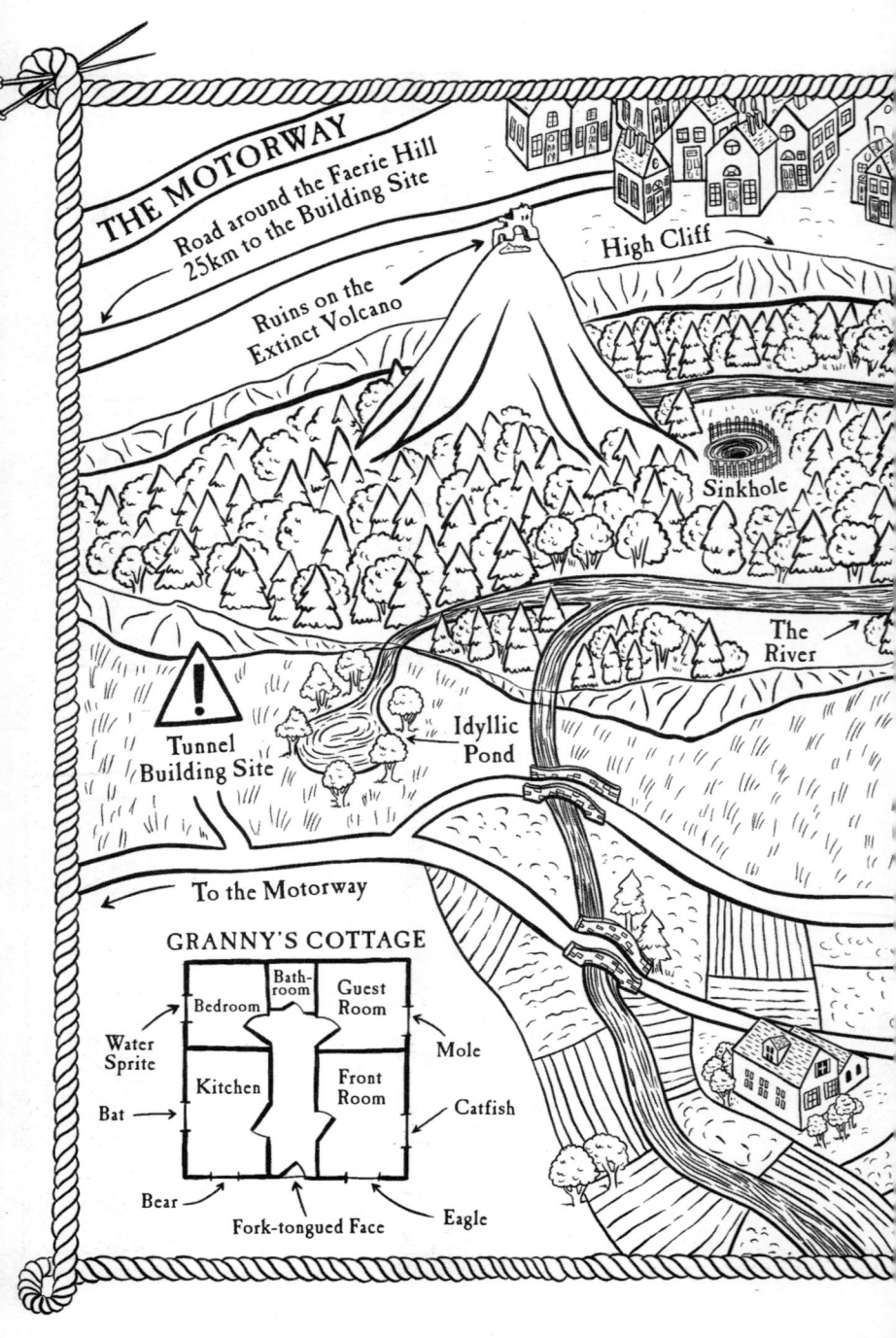

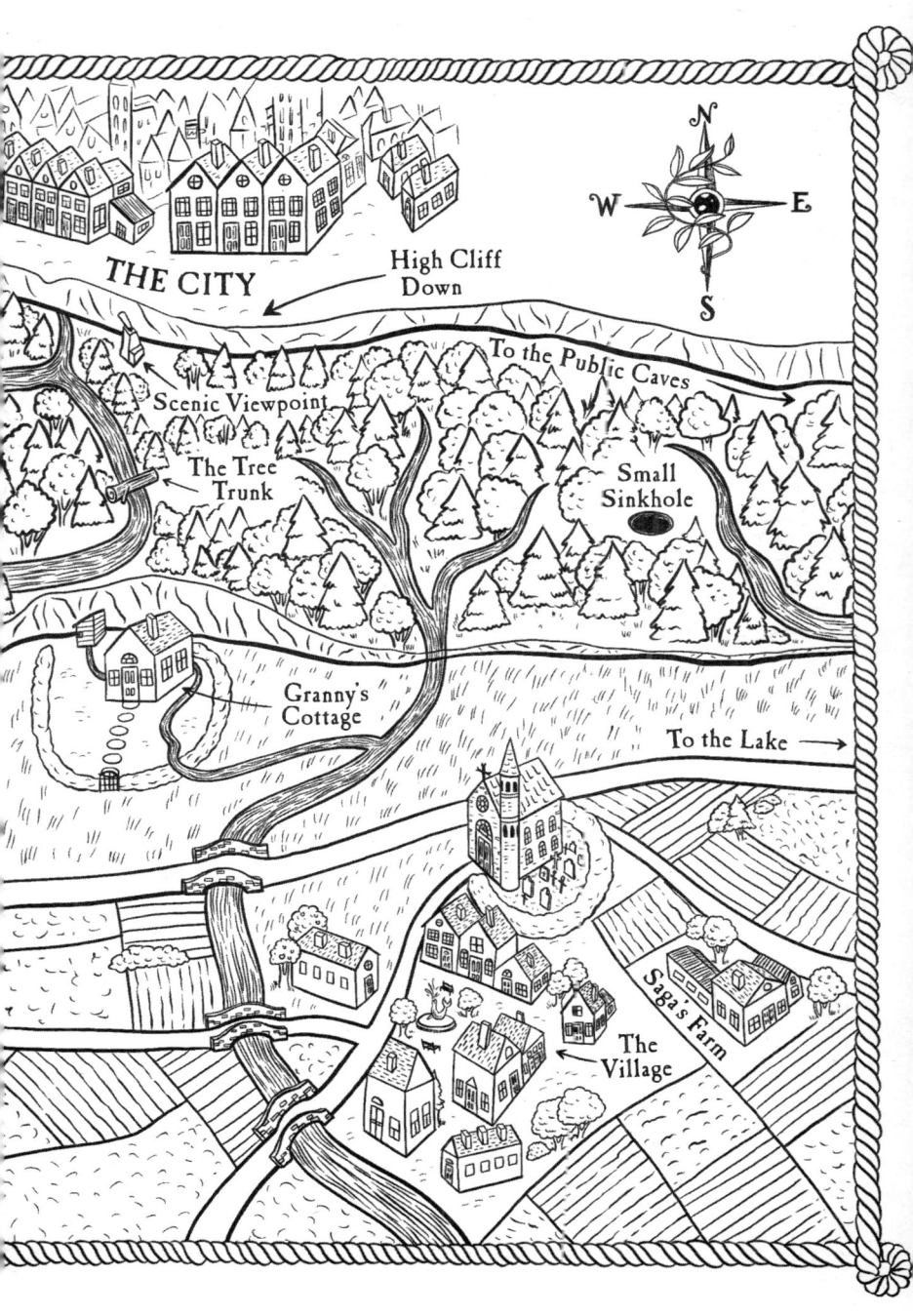

The Cottage Under the Forest

Alfred stopped on the garden path, slowed his heartbeat and concentrated on becoming invisible. He thought about his jeans turning the faded, peeling brown of the gate behind him. He focused on his T-shirt becoming a mass of sun-speckled leaves. And he imagined his dark, unruly curls becoming the twigs of a corkscrew hazel. This time, though, his little trick didn't work. It didn't make the feeling of being watched disappear.

Ahead of him, Dad was skipping towards the red door of Granny's cottage, jumping over cracked stones with easy familiarity and the movements of a carefree boy.

After closing the gate, Alfred looked up at the limestone cliff that rose behind the cottage. At the top of the cliff, tall trees leant out from the edge, stretching their branches over the thatched roof. Tree roots formed deep lines in the rock face. They looked like pointy teeth, ready to gobble the cottage in a single bite.

Alfred shuddered. Maybe all his dark-forest nightmares stemmed from here. The place was even more sinister than he recalled from his visit five years ago. He only remembered staying here once, but of course he knew that he was born in this cottage and had lived in it the first months of his life, until Dad took him away.

In the past twelve years, the two of them had lived in ten different cities, in six different countries, on three different continents. A stream of nannies had taught Alfred their mother tongues. An even bigger stream of bullies had used those languages to taunt him. Granny had travelled to visit them wherever they called home.

'Come on, Alfie,' Dad said from the front step. 'Mum, we're here!' he called, as he opened the door.

A crow cawed. Two black birds took off from the roof and swooped down towards Alfred, coming so close he ducked. The slab of granite he was standing on wobbled. He put the foot of his longest leg down on the next stone.

Something scuttled around under the hedge of brambles.

'Does granny have a cat?' he called, without getting an answer. Careful not to lose his balance, Alfred crouched and peered under the thorny branches.

'A cat? That one calls us a cat, Little Father,' a high-pitched, screechy voice said.

'Is it him, Little Mother? It is, isn't it?' a slightly less screechy voice replied.

'Hello,' Alfred said. 'Who's there?' He thought he could see a pair of eyes reflecting the light. An odd musty smell mixed with the scent of roses.

'Is he speaking to us?' the first voice, the one called Little Mother, asked.

'Never mind that. We must tell Her at once, Little Mother.'

Whatever was hiding under the brambles scuttled away. Leaves shook and white petals floated to the ground.

Alfred stood up and craned his neck. On the other side of the hedgerow, poppies and dandelions dotted a green meadow. The long grass swayed in a zigzag pattern. Clouds of downy tufts rose and blew away.

Could it have been small children? It didn't sound like children, but the grass wasn't tall enough to hide adults, and he couldn't believe anyone would be able to crawl away so fast. Perhaps talking animals? He rolled his eyes at himself. Probably it was all in his head.

Somehow, whenever he was in the countryside surrounded by nature, Alfred's imagination went into overdrive. He often had the feeling something was watching him. A few times, he'd imagined seeing glimpses of weird creatures. Once, when he'd been swimming in the sea, an ugly catfish had warned him of an undertow near the shore. Or so he'd imagined.

The cat, or whatever it was he'd actually seen just now, disappeared in the direction of the trees.

As he stepped from stone to stone, Alfred tried not to look up at the forest. He focused on avoiding the cracks and only raised his eyes as far as the cottage. The red door was open. He could hear Dad's and Granny's voices. But it was as if his gaze was being pulled upwards to the half-circle of panelled windows above the door.

Alfred gasped. A small face up there was staring back at him. He stopped abruptly, tried to still his racing heart, become unnoticeable, unseeable, invisible. It still didn't work.

The face was unnaturally long. Black, deep-set eyes narrowed. A tongue flicked out—a forked tongue.

All his nightmares came awake in his mind. His breathing grew shallow. So many times, this exact face had invaded his dreams and made him wake up screaming. He hadn't known where it came from. He hadn't remembered. But it was here, from Granny's cottage.

Quickly, his eyes sought out the panelled windows on either side of the door. Two of his other nightmare figures were there. In one window stood a carved wooden bear with its nose in the air as if it were sniffing. Its head had almost human features. In the other stood a wood-carved eagle in flight, its wings spread wide. Its eyes were clearly human, and it was scowling at him with a cold glare that gave him the chills.

Alfred glanced back up above the door. Like fun-mirrors, the old windows must've been skewing the features, because now the forked tongue was still, the eye sockets empty, and it was just a strange face carved out of a small wooden log.

He wondered if his mother had found the woodcarvings scary too. If she had liked it here...

He often wondered about his mother. Who had she been? Did he resemble her at all? Most of all, he wondered whether she'd been like Dad, someone easy-going who fitted in everywhere without having to make an effort. Or whether she'd been like him, a fish out of water, always an outsider.

The hope of learning more about her was the only reason he'd agreed to stay in the cottage.

Granny pushed past Dad out onto the front step. A strand of long dark hair had escaped her bun and swept across her forehead.

'Alfred,' she called. She didn't rush out to hug him or say any of the usual things, like how lovely it was to see him again and how much he'd grown since Christmas. Instead, she looked up and left and right with a worried frown. 'Don't stay out there. Come inside!'

'Why?'

'Don't dawdle now.'

Limping slightly, Alfred hurried the last steps.

A whisper went through the trees far above, and a flutter of leaves, like green snow, fell behind him, as Alfred entered the cottage, crossing the threshold.

2

The Forbidden Woodcarvings

Granny hugged him. Alfred was almost as tall as her now. At least, the left side of his body was. The right side, his right leg, was 5.3 centimetres shorter.

With the front door closed, the main light in the narrow hallway came from the half circle of windows above the door. On the white-washed wall behind Granny, the shadow of the rectangular shape with its forked tongue seemed to be licking the air. But the tension he'd felt outside in the garden was gone. Now it was just a carved piece of wood.

'Do you still remember your way around my castle?' Granny let go of him and pointed to the room with the wood-carved bear. 'Kitchen.' She continued moving clockwise, pointing at the remaining four doors. 'My bedroom. That's the bathroom. The guestroom. And finally, the front room.'

Alfred looked into the front room, past the eagle he had seen from the garden path. Behind a velvety armchair was a window to the side of the cottage with another wooden sculpture. From where he stood, he couldn't see what it was.

'I'll just get your suitcase,' Dad said.

Granny called something after Dad, out of the front door,

but Alfred wasn't listening. It felt like he was hooked and being pulled towards the far window. He stepped into the front room, his eyes fixed on the floor to avoid looking at the eagle. But he couldn't avoid seeing the dark V-shaped shadow its wings made on the rug by the sofa. As Alfred neared it, the shadow danced. The V-shape narrowed and widened, as if the eagle had beaten its wings.

Alfred stopped and stared at the back of the bird. The whole wooden sculpture was the size of a small cat, from the stand—a flat disc the claws gripped—to the tips of the raised wings. It didn't move.

Determined to face the carved figure right away, he reached out and grabbed hold of the stand to avoid touching the bird itself. As he turned the eagle round, his gaze slid from the smooth, pointed claws over the feathered legs to the plumage of the breast. Each individual feather was so finely carved it looked real. Above, the beak glistened in a beam of sunlight. The eyes pierced him. They seemed to stare all the way into his soul.

'Don't touch that,' Granny yelled, interrupting his thoughts. She rushed into the room and pushed past Alfred. 'It's not a toy!'

Like Alfred, she only held the stand, as she rotated the eagle until it faced the window and the garden beyond. She took care to position it exactly as it was before he'd touched it.

'Sorry,' Alfred mumbled, and hurried back to the hallway.

Granny followed him, saying, 'Please don't play with my woodcarvings. They're... kind of special.'

Alfred wanted to say that he wasn't playing with the eagle, that he wasn't a little kid who played with toys any more, and that he'd just wanted to take a closer look at it. But he didn't get the opportunity.

Dad came out of the guest room, squeezing past him and Granny.

'Change your shoes, Alfie,' he said, as he ducked under the doorway to the kitchen.

'Did you listen to the radio in the car?' Granny followed Dad. 'Another disappearance.'

Dad shut the kitchen door, but Alfred heard his muffled voice asking, 'There's been more than one?'

After a glance back at the eagle, Alfred went into the guest room. Without looking at the window sill, he sat down on the narrow bed, extracted his indoor shoes from the suitcase, and put them on.

A dresser stood in a corner of the room and a small wardrobe behind the door. Granny's enormous loom, covered by a white sheet, took up most of the remaining space. He could see the wooden frame and the foot-treadle. One of her acclaimed tapestries hung above the bed. It was an abstract, but he was almost certain it depicted a river running through a forest. A friendly forest. Light seemed to shine out from the blue-green threads of the water.

He didn't remember seeing this particular tapestry at her exhibition in Tokyo, but he liked it. Had it already been here when his mother had stayed in the room? Had she liked it?

Quietly, he opened the drawers of the dresser, one by one. They were full of yarn in all the colours of the rainbow. The wardrobe contained nothing but rolled-up tapestries and small woven samples. There wasn't anything under the bed. He even tilted the mirror on the dresser to look behind it. But there was nothing there. No trace of his mother anywhere in the room.

And why would there be?

It had been more than twelve years since she'd been here.

More than twelve years since she'd died here, a few weeks after he was born. Alfred couldn't help wonder if Dad had died a little too that day. Why else had he erased everything about Alfred's mother from his mind and turned her into a taboo subject? The mere mention of her name made him shut down any conversation and bury himself even deeper in his work.

When Granny visited, she'd avoided the subject too, but Alfred had learnt many small details from her. On one visit, she'd let slip that his green eyes were the exact same colour as his mother's—and Granny knew colours better than anyone. On another, she'd compared their olive skin tones, which were so unlike her own and Dad's pale complexions. And, whenever she saw him swimming, she always mentioned how proud his mother would've been.

His mother's name was Nereida—he knew that, without remembering who'd told him. He sometimes spoke the strange name out loud to himself before falling asleep. Saying it had become a nightly ritual, ever since Dad had said they would be moving home.

Home. It was such an odd word to use for a place he couldn't remember. As if this was where they belonged.

Alfred couldn't delay any longer. He got up to look at whatever monster was on the window sill. Without touching it, he leant over the small wooden sculpture. Like the other figures, it faced the outside, almost as if it was keeping watch.

He didn't remember the little mole that stood there from his nightmares. The tiny eyes and ears were small knots in the wood on either side of a large snout. The forepaws were oversized. Every joint and crease on the twelve digits that stuck out in front of the animal were visible. The pointed fingernails leant against the glass.

When he left the room, he heard Granny's and Dad's raised voices through the closed kitchen door.

'I told you already. He shouldn't stay here,' Granny said.

'I can move the loom.'

'It's not about the loom. You know I'm too busy colouring yarn to weave in summer. Besides, I'm going to be at the market most days.'

'Mum, please... I'll be working day and night. And you used to take me to the market all the time.'

Alfred went into the bathroom. When he closed the door behind him, he couldn't hear them any more. In pitch blackness, he searched for and found the switch. Leaning against the cool outer wall, he unlocked his phone, wanting to watch a video clip that could distract him. But his phone had no connection. He couldn't find a single Wi-Fi network either.

There wasn't a window in the bathroom, and it had to be right up against the limestone cliff. Would the cottage wall grow out of the cliff, or could there be a narrow gap behind the house?

He tried to imagine the space outside. Anything to avoid thinking about what he had overheard. But it was no use. Granny didn't want him here. Now that he thought about it, it was strange that he'd only visited once since he was a baby.

If she didn't want him here, he wanted to stay even less. He'd much rather be bored in a hotel room all day, while Dad was at work, than stay here. It had been ridiculous to think he could find a trace of his mother in the cottage—why would there be, when Dad didn't even own a photo of her?

He slammed the bathroom door so they could hear him coming. As he entered the kitchen, Granny and Dad sat at the round table, talking about whether it was likely to rain.

 3

Not Just Another Tunnel

'We've just agreed that you'll be staying here the next two weeks, Alfie. I've left a note with my new phone number and the number of the hotel, next to Granny's phone. You'll have to use the landline. There's no mobile coverage here. No internet either.'

'I know,' Alfred muttered.

Granny nodded and smiled, but Alfred noticed worry-wrinkles around her eyes and a deep frown above her specs.

'I'll start looking for a flat for us so we can get settled before the new school year begins.'

They had already talked about all this, and it was as if Dad were speaking rehearsed lines in a school play. At the thought of starting a new school yet again, Alfred's stomach clenched.

'Can I have some milk, please?' he asked.

Granny sprang up and poured him a glass. 'Remind me to put milk out later for the...' She cleared her throat. 'For the hedgehogs.'

Perhaps it had been hedgehogs he'd heard under the brambles. But hedgehogs couldn't run that fast, could they? Or speak.

'Alfie, are you listening? Granny's talking to you.'

'I was just saying that the refurbished sports centre is right next to your new school. Been in the papers a few times.' Granny passed him a plate of roast chicken with mashed potatoes, gravy and peas.

'He already knows that, Mum. Right, Alfie? I told you they have an Olympic-sized pool. That's why we chose that school, remember?' Dad reached over the table and ruffled Alfred's hair. 'They actually have a decent team, Mum. Placed second in the regionals. With Alfie on their side, they could go to nationals.'

'I don't want to join the swim team.'

'Of course you'll join the swim team,' Dad said, then turned back to Granny. 'The coach is very keen. Offered to do some trainings with him in the last two weeks before term starts.'

Alfred wished he could jump in a pool right now. He was used to training three hours daily. After weeks without swimming, he longed for that feeling of being one with the water. But swimming was one thing. Being part of a team was another. He'd tried his best at the last three schools, and it still wasn't enough. He still didn't fit in.

Just last month, he'd won every discipline except backstroke at a regional competition, and he'd had to talk to a journalist after the prize ceremony. His teammates had congratulated him. He'd felt great, and even a little sad that he was about to move away.

The interview meant he was last to enter the cafeteria, where the team sat around a table with their coach. They had been right inside the entrance. But when Alfred reached the double doors, he crouched to retie his shoelaces. That's when he heard them. Not his own team at first, but the boy who'd come second in both 1,000-metre races.

'Where's your freak?' he asked.

'On his way to the Paralympics,' Oscar from Alfred's team answered.

'Hope he doesn't have to walk to get there,' someone said, and the entire table erupted in laughter.

'Come now, boys,' Coach said, chuckling.

Alfred had stilled his breath and concentrated on becoming as uninteresting as the concrete wall behind him. It wasn't hard. He'd slipped right past them, in plain sight.

The following two weeks, until term ended, he'd feigned an injury, so he wouldn't have to attend practice. He hadn't said goodbye to anyone, and he wouldn't ever see them again—they lived on the other side of the world.

When he emerged from the memory, Alfred discovered he had made a square gravy pool in his mashed potatoes.

'I wish there was a pool for you here in the village,' Dad said.

'The Millers have a swimming pool.' Granny held a bowl towards him. 'More peas?'

'Mum. They already had that pool when I was a kid. It's eight metres long and shallow in one end. The lake would be better. It's only a thirty-minute walk.'

'Or I could just come with you to the city, to use that amazing Olympic-sized pool, and pop back to Granny's whenever you're busy. Didn't you say the city's just on the other side of the forest?'

Dad shook his head. 'There's a reason we're building a tunnel.'

'As the birds fly, the city's only four kilometres away,' Granny explained.

'But there are no roads through the forest, and the rock face on the other side is even higher than the one behind the cottage,' Dad added. 'From here, it takes almost forty minutes to drive around the entire hill to the city.'

'Thirty-five,' Granny corrected, dragging Dad into a discussion about the world's tiniest road.

Alfred almost zoned out when they argued about where Dad might save two minutes if he was driving from the headquarters of his new company in the city to the tunnel building site he had been hired to lead.

'There's a shortcut,' Granny said. 'If you take the lane at the second—'

'But the track up towards the sinkholes has been closed off, hasn't it?'

Alfred looked up from the fence of peas he was building round the gravy pool.

While they were driving here, Dad had been telling him about the geology of the region and the two cone-shaped mountains—extinct prehistoric volcanos—they could see from the car. Suddenly, Dad had stopped talking and listened intently to the radio news. The reportage had made no sense to Alfred at the time, but now some of the pieces fell into place.

'Is that the site they mentioned on the radio?' he asked. 'Did someone disappear after falling into one of those sinkholes?'

It was as if he'd said something wrong.

Granny sighed. Dad pushed his plate away, although he hadn't finished eating.

'Yes,' Dad said, and got up. 'An engineer. I'd better get going. Early start on my new job tomorrow.'

'I told you, you shouldn't have accepted that job. Nothing good will come of drilling into that hill and disturbing the...

inhabitants,' Granny said. 'Even though it's nice to have the two of you nearby,' she hastily added.

'What do you want me to say, Mum? I had to take this job. It isn't just another tunnel.'

Confused, Alfred looked from one to the other. Dad had been consulting on tunnel projects everywhere they had lived: tunnels underneath cities, tunnels through mountains and tunnels below water. He always said every project had its own challenges, but a tunnel was a tunnel. So why wasn't this just another tunnel?

4

The Girl and the Tree Sprite

Dad grabbed his phone and car keys from the table.

'I'll come with you to the car,' Alfred said. 'I think, er... my, er, lucky medal might've fallen out of my pocket onto the seat.' The old silver medal, the first medal he'd ever won, was smooth to touch and made his fingers tingle. He usually kept it in his pocket, which was also where it was right now.

'Please, let me come with you, Dad,' he said as soon as they were out of earshot.

'Alfie... The project's a mess—I'll be working round the clock. You'll be fine here for a week or two, won't you?' Dad slowed his pace to match Alfred's.

Alfred didn't answer. The back of his neck prickled. The sense of being watched was just as bad as when they'd arrived.

Outside the gate, the hedgerow blocked the view of the cottage. Alfred took a deep breath. He could see far over rolling hills clad in yellow and green and the lane that wound down between them to the lake. The water glinted and winked at him. The sight calmed him so much he almost forgot the pouncing forest above the cliff.

He was about to plead again, when a woman called out to Dad.

'So it's true. Robbie. You've actually come home.' She was walking towards them along the lane, flanked by two children.

'Did you ever leave, Vera?' Dad rounded the car and kissed the woman's cheeks.

Alfred was in doubt about his invisibility trick, so he ducked back into the garden, edged his way in between two shrubs and stilled his breath. He hoped the people hadn't been able to see him for the car. He didn't want to meet anyone yet.

The hinges of the gate squeaked. A girl walked into the garden.

'Hello,' she called. 'I saw you. I know you're here.' She rotated on the spot, searching for him.

She looked odd. On purpose, it seemed, as if she wanted to stand out. Her ginger hair was scraped into four buns—two at the top like mouse ears and two at the back. Over her striped leggings, she wore a denim skirt that was inside-out. The long white washing label fluttered like a banner at the side hem. Her round glasses and muddy hiking boots were the only things about her that didn't look out of place.

After spotting him, she smiled and came nearer.

'Hi, I'm Saga. Are we playing hide-and-seek?' The front of her red hoodie was covered in pins and badges, saying things like *Save the Forest, Global cooling now!* and *I'm an eco-warrior*.

Before Alfred could answer, several things happened at once.

The other child—if it was a child—came jumping into view. It was skinny and only about a metre high. When it landed on the third stepping stone, a cacophony of caws erupted. A swarm of black birds took off from the trees above the cottage.

On closer inspection, it wasn't a child. The little creature resembled a stick insect that had been enlarged. Its limbs were leafless twigs. The body ended in a long, rounded oval. From where Alfred stood, he could only see a slit in the side of what he supposed was the head.

The murder of crows reached the garden. Cawing, they encircled the creature in a blurring dark spiral of flapping wings.

The stick figure ignored them and sprang on. In a low growl that sounded like groaning floorboards in an old house, it grumbled, 'Can somebody stop those nasty birdies from making so much noise? This one body cannot think.'

Then the creature raised its head towards the half-circle window above the door where the fork-tongued figurine stood. It began to tremble. A choking rattle from deep in its throat creaked. Shaking and convulsing, as if in pain, it fell to the ground, even before the crows attacked.

Saga raced to the little fellow, calling, 'Mr Tumbleweed!'

She tried to pick him up, but the twiggy limbs kicked and bashed. Birds flew under her arms and pecked at the creature. They didn't seem to harm her.

'Are you going to help or what?' she yelled, turning her head back towards Alfred for a second, hitting a crow with one of her buns so it flew straight down and bumped its beak against a stepping stone. 'I need to get him away from the birds.'

Alfred emerged from the scrub. He ran at the crows, trying to shoo them away, but they didn't even change their flight patterns.

'Hold his legs. If he doesn't kick, I can pick him up.'

Alfred latched onto first one, then another of Mr Tumbleweed's legs. Saga got a better hold on his body. Together they carried the creature back towards the gate, chased by the crows. The moment they stepped out of the garden, the birds flew away, and the little body went limp.

'Is he okay?' Alfred asked.

Saga cradled the thing in one arm. She put her ear towards his little face. A knot stuck out above the gash that was his mouth. 'He's breathing. He'll recover.' She frowned and pushed her glasses, which had slid down her nose, back into place. 'I've never seen him attacked like this before.'

'What is he?' Alfred brushed lichen off his hands. The creature's legs and arms were covered in it.

'You don't see a toad, do you? I can't believe it! Everyone else thinks Mr Tumbleweed is a toad. Even Mum and my sisters.'

On the far side of the car, Dad and Saga's mum were still chatting as if nothing had happened.

'He's a faerie creature. A tree sprite or wood elf or something like that. I'm not quite sure. He doesn't speak.' She said it as if it was the most natural thing in the world. As if faeries were real.

The creature clearly wasn't human, and it wasn't an animal or an insect. Alfred didn't know a word in any of the six languages he spoke that would be a better description than faerie. Except perhaps elf or sprite, which were just as much fantasy creatures.

He thought back to a holiday by a mountain lake. In among the trees there, he'd seen unlikely animals—a large dog with antlers, a rabbit wearing a pinny, and a fox the size of a horse. When he'd tried to get closer to them, they had vanished. He'd always thought they were purely imaginary.

The creature in Saga's arms had spoken, though. He was almost certain.

'He's been with me since I was born,' Saga continued. 'Mum always says he was a gift from my faerie godmother. Perhaps one day I'll kiss him, and he'll turn into a prince!' She stared at Alfred with a frown, as if he were a bigger mystery than the weird little thing in her arms. 'I can't believe you can actually see him for what he is.' She shook her head pensively. 'It's a pity you'll be moving far away again. I think we could've been friends.'

Alfred frowned. 'Why do you think I'll be moving?'

'I'm just guessing you won't be staying when the tunnel project closes down. Will you?'

The tunnel project closes down? What was she on about?

'Oh, my!' Saga's mother exclaimed, drawing his attention. Her hand shot up to cover her mouth. 'He looks so much like her.'

Alfred ignored Saga's comment about the tunnel project and hurried over next to Dad.

'I can't believe it's been twelve years.' Saga's mother sniffed, then smiled at Alfred. 'Do you know...' she sniffed again. 'Do you know, I was the first person who ever saw you.'

'Even before I did,' Dad said. 'Vera delivered you.'

'Just two days before Saga was born. You're practically twins.'

Alfred wanted to ask how he looked like his mother, but Dad had caught sight of Mr Tumbleweed.

He stared at the creature and frowned.

'Twelve years and I'm still not used to that toad,' Saga's mum said. 'It sleeps in her bedroom and follows her around like an old, faithful dog.'

'A toad?' Dad muttered.

'Mum, some birds attacked him. Can I treat his wounds with iodine?'

'I have a witch-hazel ointment. We'd better get going. Why don't you come over tomorrow afternoon, Alfred? We're at the farm right down there, behind the chapel. The two of you played so well together last time...' Her chatter trailed off, and, after a worried glance at Dad, she said a quick, 'Bye, now.'

Alfred didn't ask Dad if he could come with him to the city.

He couldn't remember that he had played with Saga when he'd been here five years ago, although there was something familiar about her. And he didn't really want to be friends with Saga now. But Saga's mum had known his mother. She remembered his mother. And, unlike Dad and Granny, she might be willing to talk about his mother.

5

Milk for the Hedgehogs

Alfred lay awake for a long time, thinking about Mr Tumbleweed and Saga, strange creatures and attacking birds, and how the branches of trees stretched out far above him, like a tidal wave. But eventually he slept, dreaming about swimming in the river in Granny's tapestry.

After a breakfast of freshly baked bread with butter and sliced sugar-sprinkled strawberries, Granny offered to show him her shed where she was dying yarn.

Alfred followed her, thinking that she was trying her best to make him feel welcome. Perhaps staying here would be nicer than he'd thought.

But when he stepped out of the door, three crows swooped down towards the lawn. They flew in circles in front of the cottage, almost as if they wanted to keep him indoors. The feeling of unease returned.

From outside, Granny's garden shed was tiny. It was built right up against the limestone cliff. While Granny was opening the bolts, Alfred looked around.

Firewood lay stacked alongside the cliff towards the rose hedge that bordered the garden. A small axe stuck out of a tree stump scored with chopping marks. In front of the rose-bushes, pale pink dots created a stippled line on the lawn. He stepped closer and saw that the dots weren't rose petals but entire blooms.

'What happened to your roses?' he asked.

'Oh no, not my Albas! Those nasty critters!' Granny ran back into the cottage, calling, 'How could I forget?' She returned with a small ceramic dish full of milk and placed it under the rose hedge.

'Hedgehogs did this?'

Granny didn't answer. She hurried into the shed, saying, 'I hope they haven't...'

When she didn't re-emerge, Alfred followed. But Granny wasn't in the tiny shed. Instead of a back wall, a ragged opening led into the cliff.

'Thank goodness!' Granny's voice came from somewhere inside.

She popped out of the opening, saying, 'Come on,' before she pulled a metal chain.

Industrial lights blinked awake. They lit up a spacious cave, bigger than her entire cottage.

'Surprised?' she asked. 'My grandfather discovered the cave and built the shed. I used to love playing in here when I was little.'

Alfred nodded, glancing around. The harsh light cast strange shadows on the rough ceiling. 'Why didn't I see this last time?'

'It wasn't... I had other things on my mind.' Granny turned away and strode past a table with onions and beets and other vegetables scattered among baskets of dried flower petals and leaves. On the other side of the entrance stood an old gas stove with an enormous pot. A smell of soap and wet sweaters hung in the cool, stale air.

Granny pulled on rubber gloves. Alfred followed her, as she went from one trough filled with dark liquid to the next, lifting out bundles of yarn. They dripped on her colour-splashed coverall and the uneven ground. She carried some bundles outside to check their colour in daylight, before she put them back in the dye baths or hung them on hooks on a metal pole at the very back of the cave. Behind this curtain of dripping yarn, the cave grew dark and narrow. Alfred couldn't see where it ended. If it ended.

An underground spring trickled from the darkness, along the cave wall and out into the garden. He squatted and looked into the clear water. There was a ringing in his ears, like the faint echo of a choir. He stretched his hand towards the water. His fingertips hovered just above the surface. It was as if he could feel the ripples over the rocks, the energy of the current, the longing to reach the ocean.

'That's the secret to my vibrant colours. This spring is enchanted,' Granny said, 'And it's so clean you can drink the water. Try!'

Alfred stood up and crossed his arms. 'It's okay. I'm a bit cold.'

'Then go out in the sun. I still have work to do in here. Can you hang this hank on the hook outside? It should be safe now.' She passed him a thick coil of wet yarn in a greenish colour. 'And would you mind putting the Alba heads in that basket?'

Once outside, Alfred wished he'd stayed in the cave, because of the forest. Crouching, he tried to spot a hedgehog among the firewood. As he crawled along the line of blooms, gathering them in the basket, he noticed that the stems weren't bitten off. They had been cut neatly just below the heads.

When he came to the hedge, he searched under the tangles. The dish of milk was empty. The same odd musty odour he'd smelt on his arrival hung in the air. He could've sworn it hadn't been there before he went into the shed. He stilled his breath and listened.

At first, all he heard was birdsong and the rustle of leaves far above. But then there was a slurping sound and a loud belch.

'Taught her a lesson, didn't we, Little Mother,' a screechy voice said.

'That we did, Little Father, that we did.'

Whatever Granny thought, hedgehogs hadn't drunk her milk. The voices probably belonged to some kind of faeries or sprites or elves. Perhaps relatives of Mr Tumbleweed.

'I can hear you,' he said, trying to sound braver than he felt. 'Come out so I can see you.'

But the little people didn't appear, and they stopped speaking. In frustration, he threw a small stick in through a gap in the thorny tangle.

'Ouch,' a voice said.

'Sorry,' Alfred called. 'I didn't mean to hit you. Just come out here.'

'Sorry?' The leaves shook violently. 'He will be sorry, he will.'

'We'll teach that one a lesson too.' Muttering threats he couldn't hear, the voices moved further away.

Alfred shivered. He got up and carried the basket back to the shed door.

Inside, Granny hummed to herself as she worked.

On the other side of the shed, the spring came out from the cave. It trickled along the limestone wall, between the rock face and the cottage. He followed it, traipsing on a slippery path next to the stream, behind the bedroom and bathroom walls. In the narrowest part, he could touch the cliff with one hand while his shoulder brushed against the cottage.

Outside his bedroom window, he studied the little wood-carved mole. He reached up to place his fingertips against the sharp nails on the hands inside. A buzzing sounded. The glass quivered. A crow cawed. He quickly withdrew his fingers, balling them up into fists.

The next window, which brought morning sunlight into the front room, displayed a stuffed catfish. Or was it too carved from wood? Its wide flat mouth was open, the beady eyes glazed over. The whiskers were so long they reached the surface of the window sill. A creature from the depth of murky water, it was ugly but not scary.

On his way round the front of the cottage, he passed the other windows and the red door with his gaze fixed on the ground. He ducked as he rounded the corner and crept under the kitchen window at the side of the cottage, because he'd already seen the woodcarving that stood there. It was a bat.

The wood of the wings was so thin that they appeared to be almost see-through. Each tooth was carved into a sharp spike and the pointy ears seemed to be vibrating. He'd often dreamt about a cloud of bats chasing him through a forest. No doubt those nightmares stemmed from this particular bat.

There was only one window left. Granny's bedroom window. When he reached it, he took a deep breath, before he raised his eyes to the window sill.

As expected, another woodcarving stood there, facing outward. But this one was different. Not an animal. Not scary. Not the stuff of nightmares, but of dreams.

It was as small as a mouse and would fit in a hand. At first, he thought it was a mermaid, but the figure didn't have a fishtail. She sat turned sideways, and he could see her feet. An abundance of curling, flowing hair covered most of her torso and legs. A drop of resin, like a tear, glistened on one cheek. He wanted to reach out and brush the tear away.

Alfred glanced back towards Granny's shed. Perhaps he could slip into her bedroom before she'd finished with her yarn. But, just then, she came outside. Her humming stopped. She frowned, her eyes flicking from him to the window. Then she turned and closed the door, securing it with two heavy bolts, but no locks.

'Are you afraid of thieves?' Alfred asked, just to say something.

'Heavens no.' Granny chuckled, but she double-checked the bolts.

'Or your yarn escaping?'

'Something like that,' she said.

Alfred wanted to ask about the not-mermaid and why Granny had all the scary woodcarvings, instead he just said, 'I like that one.'

'So do I, dear.' Granny stepped past him. 'So do I.' He thought he heard a sniff. She seemed to hesitate for a moment, then walked round the corner of the cottage, saying, 'Time for a cup of tea, I think. Let me just get changed.'

He followed, calling out the question on his mind. 'What is it?'

Her steps slowed. Without stopping or turning, she said, 'A water sprite.'

6

No Drill into the Faerie Hill!

When they sat down for lunch, with the radio news murmuring in the background, Alfred asked, 'Where did you get those woodcarvings?'

But before Granny could answer, she sprang up and increased the volume on the radio. The speaker boomed into the little room.

'A search party of firefighters, miners and volunteers has recovered the two engineers from a hitherto unknown sinkhole. Both victims have severe concussions and several broken limbs. They appear to have been unconscious until they were brought to the hospital. It is expected that both will recover fully after their ordeal. Earlier today, we caught up with Mayor Underwood to discuss a project that has been haunted by problems and accidents from the very beginning...'

'Thank heavens.' Granny sank back into her chair. She sat staring so fixedly at the wall behind Alfred that he turned round, but there was nothing there.

The radio scratched.

A new voice spoke against a backdrop of noise. *'Mr Mayor, how relieved are you?'*

'Very relieved,' Mayor Underwood answered in a deep voice. 'The two men will no doubt be back at work soon. And the sooner we start drilling—'

Here, boos and hisses interrupted the mayor.

He raised his voice above the din. 'With Mr Applevale on board, I expect everything will run smoothly from now on.'

At the mention of Dad's name, Alfred s ears pricked.

'That odious man,' Granny mumbled. 'Why did he have to shout your father's name from the rooftops?'

The speaker elaborated. *'You're talking about international tunnel expert Robert Applevale, who has returned home after his latest successes in Italy, Canada and Japan. What does it mean to have someone with this level of expertise available for our little tunnel?'*

The mayor spluttered. *'Little! I'll have you note this is the largest infrastructure project undertaken in our entire region in the last two decades. A project I initiated in my first term of office and will see to the end. No matter what!'*

'What would you like to say to the critics and nature conservation groups who seem to have gathered here outside the hospital today?'

'They should go home and mind their own business.'

The background noise increased. Shouts of *'Protect the forest!'* and *'Save nature!'* were audible.

'We are protecting nature, by directing traffic underground!' The mayor bellowed. *'So what if a small part of the woods has to go? So what if pesky insects can't lay eggs in the pond any more? So what if a few bats have to find new limestone caves? We have nature aplenty in our county. We only have one motorway. And, with the tunnel, that motorway is going to be something people will appreciate far and wide for decades to come. In the future, they will praise me... er, us, for our foresight.'*

The crowd was baffled into silence.

A lone girl's voice yelled, *'No drill into the Faerie Hill!'* It sounded familiar.

'Is that Saga?' Alfred asked.

Granny frowned and shrugged. 'It might've been. Sensible girl. Unlike that pompous dunce.'

The mayor continued, unperturbed. *'Nothing and no one can stop this project now. We break ground in two days and drilling starts next week.'*

More shouts of *'nature'* and *'preserve'* rang out, before the studio host was back. *'Tomorrow will be another scorching—'*

Granny turned down the volume and stood leaning against the sink, looking out of the window towards her shed. 'Your father is a fool too. How can he think this won't have repercussions for all of us?'

'Do you mean they shouldn't fell the trees? Or is this about that pond the mayor mentioned? Or...' He hesitated, recalling her panic when she saw the rose heads on the lawn. She was evidently scared of something. Could it be the little people? Did she really believe she was up against a pair of cute pincushion mammals? 'Or other creatures?' he asked. 'Like... like the hedgehogs?'

'All of that.' Granny shook her head before she turned. 'Mark my words, nothing good will come of this.'

When she moved, Alfred could see the carved bat. Its ears twitched. 'And what about those bats he mentioned? Are they endangered?'

'You could say that.'

'Are they like that one?' He pointed at the bat sculpture.

Granny nodded.

'Where did they come from? Not the real bats. That wooden one and the other carvings.'

She sighed. 'Your mother gave them to me.'

'Where did she get them?' Alfred asked, just as the phone rang.

'Let's not dwell on the past. I'd better get that.' Granny answered the phone, with a cheery, 'Applevale cottage.'

Alfred half-listened to her side of the chat with what appeared to be Saga's mum. He twisted on his chair so he could see both the bat and the bear. They were about the same size, and as tall as the magazine file holder stuffed with gardening magazines that stood next to the bat. The same size as the eagle and the mole and the catfish.

Where had his mother found them? They didn't look like something you could buy in a shop. Perhaps his mother had been the one to place the woodcarvings in the windows, facing the outside. Perhaps that was the reason Granny didn't want anyone to move them around.

'Saga's home. Run along now, dear. I'll clear this up,' Granny said, and turned up the music while she started rinsing their plates.

Sitting on the stool in the hallway, Alfred changed into his sturdy high-top trainers. They were black, and it was almost impossible to see that one of their black soles was higher than the other. He glanced up at the creepy fork-tongued figurine above the front door. It was much smaller than the other woodcarvings, almost as small as the mouse-sized water sprite. Looking at it made him shudder.

He wished he could sneak into Granny's bedroom and hold the water-sprite figurine, but he never ever wanted to touch that face or its forked tongue.

7

The Empty Grave

Even if the woodcarvings were from his mother, Alfred still didn't like the way their staring eyes prickled the back of his neck. He held his breath until he'd closed the garden gate behind him.

The lane towards the farm led him past the meadow where he'd first seen something he now guessed were Little Mother and Little Father disappear up to the forest. He wondered if they lived up there or under the rose hedge.

Granny's spring ran alongside the narrow road. Its tinkling sound calmed him. Where it joined a larger stream and flowed under the lane, he stopped. From above, he watched the water rush down over rocks, spraying glittering droplets. The stream snaked across a field with grazing cows. The water from Granny's spring stood out like individual threads of a particular turquoise.

Alfred shook his head and blinked. That was impossible.

But when he looked back, he still saw the stream as intertwined layers, like yarn in blues and greens, with a finely spun turquoise standing out. The colour made him think of the water-sprite figurine, which was strange because she was the same brownish beige as the other wood-carved creatures.

Nearer to the farm, he saw that there was a graveyard by the chapel. The thought that his mother could be buried here in the village had never even crossed his mind. But where else would she be?

Quickly, he plucked a bunch of poppies at the edge of the meadow.

Inside the graveyard hedge, an old man wearing a faded cap was whistling and weeding next to a wheelbarrow.

Alfred paused. He slowed his breath and heart rate, and focused on blending in with the colours of the slightly wilted hedge, before he sneaked right past the old man.

His invisibility trick worked for once.

To minimize the crunching sound of the gravel, he tiptoed. He read the names on the gravestones, hoping that he would find his mother's name, at the same time as he hoped he wouldn't. It was silly, of course. He knew she was dead, but there had always been a tiny flicker of hope, a sense that she was still somewhere in the world.

When he was little, he'd imagined she was held prisoner by a witch or a dragon or perhaps sleeping behind a wall of thorny roses. Later, he daydreamt that she was searching for him, but couldn't find him because they kept moving. And he couldn't count the times, on especially rotten days, that he had wished she would suddenly turn up, waiting for him by the school gate or when he came out of the changing rooms after swimming. These wishful thoughts included no explanation of where she had been all these years. The fairy tale always ended when she took him into her arms.

Alfred didn't register any of the names until he found hers.

Nereida Applevale.

He read the inscription through a blur of tears. *Beloved wife, mother, sister*, it said below a date. A sob escaped him. But something was wrong. Alfred wiped at the tears with the sleeve of his T-shirt.

The year was wrong.

According to the inscription, she hadn't died just after he was born. She had died five years ago, twelve days after he turned seven. Why had Dad told him something else? Where had she been hiding in those seven years? And who was the sister? He didn't have any aunts.

Alfred sank to his knees, crushing the poppies below his hand. He kept staring at the inscription, and then glanced at the gravestones left and right. Something else was odd.

'Where did you come from?' a gruff voice asked. The old man stood, looking down at him.

Alfred had forgotten to stay invisible, and now it was too late.

'Wouldn't waste flowers on that grave,' the man wheezed.

'What do you mean?'

'Coffin was empty. Isn't the only one either. No one thinks of the one who has to dig the grave with this kind of antics.' He wiped his forehead with a stained handkerchief. 'Seems a waste to pay for a plot, but that Mrs Applevale was always away with the faeries.'

'The grave is empty, you mean? Nereida...' It felt strange, saying the name out loud for others to hear. 'Nereida isn't dead?'

'Never said she wasn't dead. But they never found no body, did they?' The man heaved at the handles of his wheelbarrow.

'They never found a body?' Alfred sprang up, blocking the old man from moving. 'Where were they searching?' he asked, because the question of when she might've died was too confusing.

'All I know is that they poked about up there.' The man turned and his crooked, grubby finger pointed up at the dark forest behind the meadow. 'Even had a search party lowered into some sinkholes, like they did this week. Mind you, that place is like Swiss cheese. Don't think they'll need much drilling and dynamite to make that blasted tunnel.' With a wheezing chuckle, the man steered round him and walked away.

Alfred shuffled back to the grave.

It was tidy. Rose bushes flowered on both sides. Directly in front of the stone, a seaweed-like plant Alfred didn't know swayed in the breeze. He nipped off a decaying rose, prickling his finger on a thorn. While sucking the drop of blood, he looked back at the inscription, recalling the other odd detail he'd noticed.

Unlike most of the gravestones, this one, his mother's, didn't include her birthday.

He glanced up at the forest. What if his mother was still up there? No, not up there. Somewhere else. Not dead. Alive.

For a brief moment, it felt like his chest would burst with hope.

Then reality kicked in. If she were alive... It didn't matter that he and Dad had moved around. She knew where Granny lived. She could've found them.

She hadn't died after giving birth. Instead, after a few weeks of being a mother—his mother—she'd had enough. His mother hadn't loved him. She'd left him.

Had she returned five years ago? And then gone missing in the woods?

It was a long while before Alfred got up.

He thought about calling Dad. But Dad always deflected his questions and said something like, 'It's no use living in the past, Alfie. Your whole life's ahead of you. You must start living it.' As if he did that himself. He just worked. And lied.

Alfred didn't feel much like visiting anyone, but he was expected at the farm anyway, and he had to talk to Saga's mum. She would know about his mother's disappearance.

8

Protest Placards

When Alfred saw the farm, he recognized it.

Three buildings stood in a horseshoe shape round a cobbled yard with an enormous chestnut tree. The nearest buildings had few windows and large doors and appeared to be barns. They framed the rainbow-coloured farmhouse.

'Give it back!' someone shouted from inside the house. Its uneven, yellow walls sagged under a red, tiled roof. Bright blue window frames were half-hidden by boxes of hanging flowers that gave everything a pinkish-green tinge.

Three barefooted children shot out of the open door, chased by a big brown dog. They ran straight through a mound of wellies and old trainers.

From behind an even bigger mound of bicycles in varying stages of rusting, a gaggle of geese appeared and broke into a noisy cackle. The dog barked.

Alfred stopped under the chestnut tree and stared at the chaotic scene.

Saga was last of the children and biggest. The group ran round Alfred and the tree. Before they reached the corner of one barn, Saga caught up with the other two. After a scuffle and some name-calling, she rose, holding a notebook close to her chest.

'Hi, Alfred,' she called.

'Hi, Alfred!' the two smaller girls chorused and ran towards him. The barking dog chased them. The geese flapped away in alarm. Their ginger plaits bounced up and down, as the girls sprinted past him and through a gap between the farmhouse and one of the barns.

'My sisters,' Saga said, when she reached him. She half-heartedly brushed dirt off her inside-out gym shorts.

Alfred looked at the notebook in her hand. *Faerie Investigation Society* it said in swirly letters on the front.

The leaves above them rustled. Twigs snapped. Saga looked up, then pushed Alfred so hard he landed on his back with her on top of him. A split second later, a large tree branch crashed to the ground in the exact spot where Alfred had been standing.

'Hold this!' Saga thrust the notebook into Alfred's hands before she sprang up. Like a monkey, she climbed the tree.

While looking up, Alfred got to his feet, prepared to jump back if that became necessary.

'Mr Tumbleweed!' Saga called. 'Come down this instant.'

Alfred tried to spot the strange creature he'd seen the previous day, but it was too well camouflaged.

He glanced down at the notebook in his hand. He didn't mean to look inside, but his thumb was between two pages, and he just peeked at that spread.

One page was full of scrawled notes. The other contained a carefully drawn map. A trail snaked diagonally across the page. It connected two black circles marked with arrows and *SINKHOLE* in capital letters. Somewhere in the middle, it crossed a river, coloured in blue. Before he snapped the notebook shut, he noticed a tiny, winged creature above one of the sinkholes and a scrawled *Faerie entrance?*

'What were you doing up there?' Saga climbed down, followed by the tree sprite. 'Did you do this?' She held onto the little creature and pointed at the branch.

It was difficult to read Mr Tumbleweed's expression. His face resembled a gnarled piece of firewood, but Alfred had a feeling he smiled.

'Just because somebody happened to be sitting in a tree, that doesn't mean that anybody can just blame that one body for anything that happens,' Mr Tumbleweed grumbled. 'The nasty somebodies said he would be sorry.'

'You can at least nod or shake your head,' Saga said, as if the tree sprite hadn't spoken.

Hadn't she heard him? Alfred frowned. Had he imagined the strange groaning voice? He couldn't have. But what did it mean if he could hear the tree sprite when Saga couldn't?

Ignoring them, Mr Tumbleweed started dragging the branch across the farmyard.

'I wish I knew what was going on in his head. Are you okay?'

Alfred nodded and handed Saga her notebook.

She led him into the house through a boot room. Layers of coats and sweaters hung on hooks and bulged out from the wall above a higgledy-piggledy collection of sandals and trainers. A burnt smell permeated the air.

'The cake!' Saga ran into the kitchen, jumped over a black cat and tore the oven open. With a pair of oven gloves, she extracted a sheet pan with something almost black and placed it on a long wooden dining table. One end of the table was full of sticky bowls, flour, sugar, cocoa powder, eggs and an empty bag of wine gums. The other end looked like an unsupervised arts-and-craft workshop had taken place.

'It'll be fine.' She scraped the worst of the charred surface and a couple of blackened wine gums into the sink.

'Isn't your mum home?' Alfred asked.

'She's out. Delivering a baby. Dad's ploughing.' While she talked, Saga poured milk from a glass bottle into four mugs and cut large slices of the cake. 'I'm babysitting until the girls are being picked up for their play date.' She rolled her eyes.

'When's your mum coming back?'

'When the baby's been born.' Saga placed two full plates on the window sill, opened the kitchen window and yelled, 'Poppy! Daisy! Cake!'

Almost immediately, to the sound of giggles, two sets of hands appeared and snapped away the plates and mugs.

Mr Tumbleweed sat in a corner, teasing the cat with a ball of yarn on an elastic band.

Alfred stepped closer to the jumble of craft supplies. Someone had been making placards. Large letters cut out in coloured paper had been glued onto pieces of cardboard.

No drill into the Faerie Hill, it said on the one on top. He could only see part of the placards below, but they were all about nature and bats and woodland biodiversity.

The faerie investigation society notebook lay next to the placards.

Saga handed him a plate and a mug. 'The milk's fresh from this morning.'

Alfred braved a bite. The cake wasn't as bad as it looked. The chewy or charred—depending on their placement—wine gums were like surprise globs or crispy bits in the sticky chocolate.

A lump of chocolate goo stuck in Alfred's throat, so he drank a gulp of milk. It tasted nothing like the milk he was used to. It was creamier, but there was also something else... He could taste the turquoise threads in the spring water the cows had been drinking. Alfred pushed the mug away.

'What's in your notebook?' he hurried to ask.

'The rules for the society and everything about faerie creatures. Oh, you should join! I'd even let you be a founding member.'

Alfred wondered how many members the society had already. He suspected he might be the second.

'I've found loads of facts in books—things you should and shouldn't do to protect yourself among faeries. For instance, you should always wear something red, bring something made of iron, and have a piece of clothing inside-out. Mr Tumbleweed doesn't count because I reckon he's here to protect me.'

'But why do you need protection? Aren't they little creatures with wings and faerie dust?' Alfred cast a glance at the tree sprite, who looked up and scowled at him.

'Which fairy tales have you read?' Saga lowered her glasses and narrowed her eyes. 'All creatures from the faerie realm—elves, sprites, pixies, goblins, shapeshifters, you name it—are faeries of some kind. A few of them might be harmless and mainly care about protecting nature, but others are dangerous and steal children or lure people into their realm. And if you end up in Faerie, you'll never escape. They'll force you to dance for all eternity, and you won't even know because you'll have no idea how much time has passed. At least that's what I've read.' She pushed her glasses back up on the bridge of her nose. 'And by the way, you shouldn't have eaten the cake without making absolutely sure that I'm not a faerie.'

'But I know that you're not.'

'And what if Mr Tumbleweed had made it?'

'Then I would've eaten a fairy cake.' Alfred grinned at his own joke. Although he wouldn't dare eat anything Granny's so-called 'hedgehogs' had prepared.

'You have a lot to learn.'

For a few moments, there was an awkward silence. Then Alfred pointed at the topmost placard.

'I heard you shout that on the radio,' he said. 'That was you, wasn't it? With the mayor.'

'You heard me?' Saga asked, a big smile spreading across her face.

'Loud and clear.'

'Good! Why on earth is your dad working on that project?'

Alfred shrugged. Was Dad there to search for a missing person? He couldn't tell Saga about his mother. He barely knew her, and she would probably think he was strange.

'Anyway, now that you're here, you can help.' She wiped her hands on her shorts and picked a bamboo stick up from the floor. 'Hold this.' After lifting the first placard aside, she turned the next sheet of cardboard over and slathered it with a generous amount of glue. Then she took the stick from Alfred and placed it so half of it stuck out at the bottom. They placed the first placard on top, making sure the cardboard sheets aligned, and dabbed until they stuck together.

'Great,' Saga said, lifting the placard and swirling it around so Alfred could see the text was the same on the other side. 'Let's do the others.'

'What are the placards for?' Alfred asked, while they worked.

'Didn't you hear the mayor? They plan on breaking ground on Friday. Obviously, we're going to stop them.'

'We are?'

A car honked outside.

'Perfect timing.' Saga pressed the last two sheets together. 'Wait here,' she said and ran out the door. 'Poppy, Daisy,' she called, 'don't forget your swimsuits!'

A moment later, he heard the car drive away, and Saga returned to the kitchen. She hurriedly stacked all the used bowls and spoons in the sink. 'D'you want more to drink before we leave?'

Alfred felt as if he'd been caught up in a tornado. Although he wanted to get home so he could ask Granny about his mother's grave, he couldn't leave now. Saga was on a mission, and her enthusiasm was contagious.

'Where are we going?' he asked.

'We need to scope out the tunnel building site.'

9

Disturbers of Peace

'You can borrow my mountain bike and helmet, while you're here.' Saga freed the nearest bicycle from the heap. It was green and looked quite new. A helmet dangled from the saddle. 'I prefer Mum's anyway.' She dragged out a rusty women's bicycle and called, 'Mustardseed!'

Mr Tumbleweed came trudging out of the house. He jumped into the basket that hung from the handlebars on Saga's mum's bike. His twiggy legs dangled out. He was the opposite of soft and gooey. Alfred couldn't understand why anyone saw a toad when they looked at him.

'Why did you call him Mustardseed?' he asked while he secured the helmet.

'Mustardseed, Tumbleweed, somebody has brains the size of a bead,' the creature grumbled.

'That's his real name,' Saga said. 'When I discovered he was a faerie creature and not a toad, I asked Mum for a faerie name. But I always call him Mr Tumbleweed when we're outside the house. Obviously.'

'Somebody should tell everybody that isn't the name for this one body,' Mr Tumbleweed groaned.

Alfred looked from him to Saga. Apparently, she hadn't heard anything. Was it all in his head? 'And no one can see what he is? Except you and me?'

'Strange, isn't it? I mean, strange that you can see he's a faerie creature.'

Alfred thought it was even stranger that he could hear the tree sprite if Saga couldn't. 'And you've never heard him speak?' Alfred asked, staring at the creature.

'No, he can't.'

'Just because somebody can't hear this one body speaking—'

'What's that sound then?'

'Oh, that's just his joints creaking. I think he might be quite old.' Saga set off, so Alfred didn't hear what Mr Tumbleweed grumbled this time, but he could guess.

They cycled along the road past the chapel and Granny's house. The sun shone. Bees hummed from poppies to dandelions and cornflowers. Behind the fields, the forest rose on the steep incline, dark and forbidding.

Birds of prey circled above the trees. One of them spiralled downwards. It was huge. Was it an eagle? Alfred had a feeling it was staring right at him, before it screeched and flew back over the woods.

He wasn't used to cycling, but it felt good to be outside with the wind in his face. The last two places he'd lived, smack bang in the centre of big cities where Dad had worked on underground railways, there had been too much traffic to cycle and excellent public transportation. Here, a bus stopped by the chapel four times per day and only twice on the weekends. So far, only one car and two tractors had passed them.

Soon, Saga stopped by a blocked-off side road. She pointed down past several fields to where a motorway snaked through the rolling hills. 'That's supposed to come up here and through the tunnel.' The droning sound of distant cars was like the buzzing of lazy wasps.

They pushed their bikes round the blockade and followed the gravel road uphill.

'This way first.' Saga led him off the road onto a trail. When they reached a cluster of trees and bushes, they left their bicycles. She took a canvas bag from the basket and swung it across her body. Alfred crawled after her and Mr Tumbleweed through a hollow in the undergrowth.

'Isn't it beautiful?' she said, when he emerged. She was already sitting cross-legged in a patch of sunlight by a large pond. Mr Tumbleweed was climbing up into the nearest tree—a weeping willow. Its hanging branches cast shifting shadows over pink and white waterlilies in the pond. 'Isn't it horrible that they'll ruin this peaceful place with that stupid motorway coming right through here?' She rustled the reeds and a frog or a toad croaked. A pair of mallards paddled out into open water.

Alfred sat down next to her and nodded.

Right in front of them, water splashed into the air. A small brown head popped up.

'Look!' Saga said. 'An otter.'

Round black eyes peeked at them, before the otter ducked and its elegant shape glided away. Underneath it, weaving between the long seagrass, turquoise threads danced.

'Can you believe they're going to fill the pond and pave over it? They'll fell the trees too—the willows, the alders, the birches, the elderberries. All the insects and the birds and the other animals that live here will lose their homes.'

Alfred took everything in. Long-limbed insects skated on the water's surface. Electric-blue dragonflies swarmed between flittering butterflies above. Grasshoppers chirped. Unseen birds sang. The air buzzed with life. And the brook that trickled into the pond made the sweetest music of all. If he was a bird or a fish and lived here, he wouldn't ever want to move.

He took a deep breath of fragrant air mixed with the pond's slightly muggy scent of still water. How could Dad be part of ruining a place like this? Did he even know this nature paradise was here?

'The worst part is that we don't know what will happen if this place is destroyed,' Saga said. 'What if a particular insect that hatches here keeps the whole ecosystem in balance? Perhaps there are birds that only nest in weeping willows— and these are the only ones in the area. What if the rare bats are extinguished because we ruin their habitat? We have to protect their world!'

Alfred was about to ask if the bats lived inside the hill, when Mr Tumbleweed fell out of the weeping willow. He landed on top of Saga. A twig at the end of his arm snapped. The little creature convulsed on the ground, groaning, 'Somebody get those nobodies away from this one body.'

'Oh no,' Saga said. 'There must be other faeries nearby.' She cradled the tree sprite and ran away, along the side of the pond.

From the tree, Alfred heard a screechy voice say, 'You missed again, Little Father. But you broke a twig on the sprite.'

'I twigged that.' Little Father chuckled. 'Get it? Twigged.'

Alfred tugged the hanging branches aside. For the first time, he saw the little people.

They were rat-sized and stocky and looked a bit like miniature garden gnomes. Their old-fashioned clothes were so filthy he couldn't tell if the greenish-brown was the original colour or just a mix of dirt and grass stains. The little woman's hair was hidden under a white-and-green chequered scarf. A green sock-like hat, with holes in the side for his pointy ears, was pushed so far down over the little man's head that all Alfred could see was a large round nose and a shaggy grey beard.

'Hurry,' Little Mother squeaked. Her long skirt with its pinny swirled as the creatures scuttled further up into the tree.

'I saw them,' Alfred said, when he'd caught up with Saga. She was sitting on the grass, scribbling in her notebook, right next to where the brook gurgled into the pond. For a brief moment, all he could hear was the plinks of its music. 'I think they pushed Mr Tumbleweed out of the tree on purpose. Did you hear them?'

'No,' Saga said, sighing. Her notebook was open to a page with a sketched map of the pond. She'd drawn a cross and written 'faeries' in the spot they'd just left. 'I never see them or hear them. I just know there are other faeries nearby when Mr Tumbleweed reacts like this.' She patted the tree sprite, who lay splayed on the ground with his head on one of her legs.

'You've never seen or heard other faeries?' Alfred asked, incredulous. He thought she knew all about them. 'Who are they? Little Mother and Little Father?'

'I just said, I don't know.'

'I'm not asking you. I'm asking him.'

'He can't speak.'

'He can! I've heard him.' Alfred reached down until he was almost touching Mr Tumbleweed. 'Tell me who they are.'

'Somebody—' The creature jerked up, then fell to the ground, his twiggy limbs flailing. He groaned, 'Aspy, aspy, aspy.' Whatever that meant.

'Stop it. You're hurting him!' Saga yelled.

'I didn't touch him.' Alfred leant back and looked up, surveying the trees, looking for the little people. He could neither see nor hear them. But something moved on the nearest trunk.

It looked like a face, with a tongue sticking out. Like the face above Granny's door.

He wanted to run away, but instead he stepped closer.

It wasn't a face. Just three knots in a triangle. A crack in the bark pointed downward from the bottom knot.

When he turned back, Mr Tumbleweed was calm. Saga had packed her notebook away.

'The faeries must be just as angry as we are about the tunnel,' she said. 'Perhaps that's why they attacked Mr Tumbleweed. To get our attention or something.'

'Isn't it better for them if the traffic is underground? Under their forest?'

'I think they live below ground. Imagine if someone drilled a hole right through your living room... Or perhaps they get to their realm through the underground, and all the caves and tunnels and sinkholes might collapse when the drilling starts.'

'Sinkholes,' he muttered. There it was again, that word.

'My theory is that you can get to Faerie through one of them.'

'Though a sinkhole?'

Saga nodded.

Alfred wondered what a sinkhole looked like. If they had anything to do with his mother's disappearance. But he didn't want to think about that now.

'Where's the tunnel site?' he asked.

In answer, loud grating sounds and the rumble of heavy machinery drowned out the music of the pond. The building site must be close, and the workers back from a break.

Saga said something he couldn't hear for the noise, before she shouted for him to follow.

Side by side, they climbed the hillock behind the pond. And just on the other side of it, the tunnel building site lay spread out below them.

Hidden behind a boulder, they watched as bulldozers, caterpillars, dumptrucks and roadrollers worked. They were clearing and flattening a large gravel plane. Three excavators stood near a massive mound of rubble. Two shipping containers with doors and windows had been stacked to form a temporary office next to the mound. Beyond the mound, a steep white cliff, like the one behind Granny's cottage, rose up to the forest.

Saga pointed at it and shouted. 'That's where they're planning on digging into the hill. We must stop them. So we're going to need people—lots of people. You'll help me recruit them.'

It didn't sound like a question, but Alfred nodded. 'People for what?' he shouted back.

'For the protest!'

10

A Sinkhole Disappearance

When Alfred returned to the cottage garden, crows descended from the trees and circled above him. Some of them landed on the lawn.

Granny was in her shed. Through the open door, he could hear her humming a tune and the splashes as she wrung out bundles of yarn. He tried to focus on those sounds and ignore the uncanny feeling that he was being observed by birds, nightmarish woodcarvings and small spiteful faeries.

In the kitchen, the table was set, and a creamy pasta dish bubbled in the oven. While he drank a glass of water from the tap, he looked out of the window. More crows arrived and settled on top of the shed. Trying to count them, he leant against the windowpane. A tiny movement in the glass caught his attention. The reflection of the bat quivered. Alfred glanced down, but, of course, the small wooden sculpture was still.

Perhaps now, before Granny came inside, was the time to examine the carving in her window—the water sprite.

Her bedroom contained a bed, a bedside table, a wardrobe and a chest of drawers. The window was open a crack, so he would be able to hear when she bolted the shed door. But the window sill was empty. Where was the figurine?

He was about to open the wardrobe when he caught a glimpse of it, hidden behind the lamp on the bedside table. In five steps, he was there, kneeling by the water sprite.

Carefully, ever so carefully, he reached his index finger towards the resin tear. Featherlight, he touched it. Then he ran his fingers over the long hair that flowed like a river all the way to the feet.

Something was slightly off with the proportions of the figurine. No one had hair this long. And the way she sat sideways with both legs bent at an angle, and the tiny feet, one directly on top of the other, also looked somehow wrong. The one ear that was visible tapered into a point. His own pointy ears looked round compared to this. He kept running his fingers down over the flowing hair, which seemed to soften under his touch. The tear glinted in the light from the window. A warm feeling deep inside relaxed him.

When Granny banged the two bolts into place, Alfred woke, as if from a trance. He had no idea how long he had sat there, mesmerized by the figurine.

On hands and feet, he scrabbled into the hallway. He looked out above the bat wings in the kitchen window, in time to see Granny turn back to her shed and double check the bolts.

'Oh, you're back. Good,' she said when she entered the cottage. 'Dinner's ready. Let me just wash.'

As soon as they sat down and she'd served the food, Alfred spoke, saying, 'I found my mother's grave today.'

Granny's fork stopped on the way to her mouth. A look of pain came into her eyes. She hesitated before her fork continued. After chewing very slowly, she asked, 'Did the roses need pruning?'

It wasn't the question he'd expected. 'Yes. No. I don't know.'

'I'll see to it tomorrow,' Granny said. 'Ah, no. I'll be at the market all day tomorrow and at the weekend. Would you like to come?'

'Er... I'm going with Saga to the lake.' Granny might not be happy about the tunnel, but he wasn't sure he should tell her they were going to the lake to recruit people for the protest.

'Oh, good. I didn't think you'd enjoy selling yarn and shawls. I don't particularly. But in summer, with all the tourists... Well, it pays the bills. I'd rather be swimming too. You must be looking forward to that.'

Just like Dad, whenever Alfred asked about his mother, Granny tried to change the subject. But he wouldn't let her.

'About the grave...' he began, then paused, suddenly unsure. He took a bite of pasta and bacon. Had Dad actually told him his mother died when he was a newborn? Or was that a story he'd been telling himself? Had he simply not listened or understood when Dad told him the truth? It was a long time since they had talked about his mother. He would start with an easier question. 'It said "sister" on the gravestone, but Dad's never mentioned that I have an aunt. Who is she? Does she live nearby?'

'I don't know, dear. Never met her. I don't think your father did either.'

'Didn't she come to the funeral?' He glanced at Granny, seeing worry spread out from her eyes.

'No.'

'Why?'

'I don't know. It's better not to dwell on the past, dear. Aren't you hungry? You used to love my cheesy bacon macaroni. But maybe you prefer Asian food now?'

'No, it's still my favourite. Saga had baked a cake,' he said to explain why he wasn't hungry, although they'd eaten cake hours ago.

'Oh, dear. Was it a madhouse over there, as usual?'

He nodded, but he wouldn't let her change topic. 'An old man—I think the gravedigger—told me—'

'Ha! Don't believe a word that old geezer tells you. All his superstitious tales about ghosts and three-legged horses in the graveyard and portents of death. Can you believe he once told some buyers who were asking for directions to the cottage that I was a witch who wove magic spells into my tapestries? Complete nonsense. Why would I need magic when the spring gives me glamour?'

But now Alfred had had enough. The gravedigger's tales could be true for all he cared. None of that mattered. He wanted to know if his mother had died when he was seven. If he'd been told, he would've remembered.

'But the date on the gravestone isn't nonsense, is it? Dad never told me she only died five years ago. And the gravedigger said the coffin was empty. Is that one of his tales?'

Granny sighed. 'You really ought to hear this from your father...'

'Then I'll call him right now.' Alfred pushed his chair back and got to his feet.

'No. Wait. It's not something one should hear over the phone. Sit down. Please.'

In the silence that followed, Alfred's chair scraped against the floorboards and creaked when he sat. The clock in the front room ticked. Granny reached across the table and put her hand over his. She cleared her throat.

'When you were twelve days old, your mother went for a walk in the woods, and she never returned. They... We searched everywhere... All the sinkholes... Below all the cliffs...'

'Was she unhappy?'

'I don't remem—'

'Please try to remember.'

Granny looked so sad, he almost couldn't bear it. But he had to know.

'No, she wasn't unhappy. She was worried about something... Oh, I don't quite recall. It's all a bit of a blur. None of us were sleeping. We kept searching long after the official search had been called off—she went on all the missing persons lists, of course—and there was you to take care of...'

'She just disappeared?'

'The assumption was that she'd fallen into one of the sinkholes and wandered into a cave or a tunnel, and then there had been a rockfall... They tried opening tunnels that looked as if they'd recently caved in. Your father was there, working tirelessly with a crew of miners. Two of them were seriously injured in a new rockfall, before they gave up.'

'But what if she ran away? She could still be alive.'

Granny shook her head. 'With all the modern technology, it's almost impossible to disappear in this day and age. After seven years without a trace, she was declared dead. Presumption of death, it's called.'

'So that's why the date...'

Granny nodded. 'And she wouldn't have run away. They were so in love. Nereida would never have left your father. Or you,' she added, as an afterthought.

'And that's why we were here five years ago... for the funeral.'

'Yes. Saga's father was looking after you during the service and afterwards... Do you remember playing with Saga?'

'I think I remember the farm.' Alfred was certain he hadn't seen Mr Tumbleweed then. That, he would've remembered.

Later, when he lay in bed and looked up at the tapestry with the turquoise river, it reminded him of the water-sprite figurine and gave him the same warm feeling deep in his stomach. Maybe the gravedigger had been right too, when he said Granny wove magic into her tapestries. Or glamour, as she called it. A calming spell, perhaps, although it couldn't quite rid him of all the gnawing questions. Today, he'd discovered so much about his mother, but instead of satisfying him, he only felt more hungry for answers.

Why had she been worried? Was it because of him? Why had she gone into the woods, and what had happened to her there?

His mind kept returning to one thought—he couldn't decide if it was positive or negative. Granny had said it was almost impossible to disappear. And he agreed. It was probably impossible to disappear in the real world. But what if Saga was right? What if there was an entry to another place up in that forest? What if his mother wasn't dead, but somehow lost after accidentally wandering into Faerie?

Was that the reason Dad had taken this job? Did he want to look for her with the enormous drill that could bore right through the Faerie Hill?

As all these questions swirled round in his head, they coalesced into one overriding desire. Alfred would do anything, go anywhere, to find out what had happened to his mother.

11

The Little People's Revenge

A scream woke Alfred the next morning. At first, he thought he'd dreamt it, but then Granny yelled, and the front door slammed.

'What happened?' he called, while he hurried to tie his shoelaces and grab the nearest T-shirt. He pulled it on, as he ran out of the cottage in boxers and shoes.

'What happened, Granny?' he repeated outside, by the door to the shed. She was running her hands through her long hair and shaking her head.

'I don't understand,' she said, and sank to her knees. 'I didn't forget the milk.'

On the grass, in front of her, lay a mound of intertwined yarn. Alfred could see at least five different colours. At least five hanks of yarn. All tangled together. There were huge colourful knots.

'Who did this?' he asked, crouching next to her, although he had a pretty good idea about the culprits. 'And don't say hedgehogs because hedgehogs couldn't do this.' He looked from under the rose hedge, where the empty dish of milk was visible, to the spring that trickled out from the side of the shed right by the cliff. 'I guess hedgehogs might be able to get into and out of the shed via the spring, but they couldn't carry yarn with them. Can they even swim?'

'Hedgehogs are excellent swimmers,' Granny muttered. She gathered all the yarn up in her arms and carried the heap to the nearby garden table.

Alfred followed and stood across from her, watching her closely. She caught him staring. Their eyes locked. Neither of them spoke. Did she know who was responsible? Was she wondering the same thing about him?

'This is going to sound strange, dear,' she finally said. 'You might think I've lost my marbles... But there are creatures here... vicious faeries—'

'I know, Granny. I've seen them. They cut off those Alba roses. Little Mother and—'

'Little Father,' they said together.

'Oh, this makes things so much easier.' Granny smiled.

'You can see them too?'

She nodded. 'It's been years—they're good at hiding—but I hear them.'

'And they really are faeries?'

'Pixies, I think, of the most malicious kind. They retaliate if I forget their milk or do something else to upset them. Not sure what I've done this time...'

'I'm sorry. It might've been me. Yesterday, I threw a stick after them into the rose hedge.' Alfred went on to tell her about the branch that had nearly fallen on him at Saga's, and how the little people had pushed Mr Tumbleweed down, trying to hit him.

'Mr Tumbleweed... Is that the ghastly faerie creature that follows Saga around?' She shuddered.

Alfred nodded and pointed at the tangle. 'I'm really sorry about your yarn.'

'It's my own fault, dear. I should've told you. I just didn't think you had the sight.' Granny glanced at her watch. 'I must get going... But first, we need to make sure you're protected. The lake should be fine. Just stay away from the forest. Come along. I'd better take that indoors to keep it safe.' She strode ahead with long threads from the heap trailing after her.

'So they can't get into the cottage?' Alfred asked.

'No. I think the woodcarvings prevent them. Not sure how.'

Alfred tucked that bit of information away so he could think about it later. His mother had given Granny the carved creatures. Did that mean she'd been able to see the faeries too? Somehow that made it more likely she'd disappeared into the faerie realm.

'What about Dad? Can he see them?'

'He used to have the sight.'

'And now? Can you lose the sight when you grow up?'

'I don't know. There's no manual for this kind of thing.' She deposited the tangle on the sofa. 'We can unravel that tonight. Now, let's see. Have you got something red? A T-shirt, perhaps. And we need iron...'

Alfred went into the guest room and came back with a red T-shirt and his old silver medal, which obviously wasn't made of silver. 'Will this do?'

Granny rummaged in a drawer and found a horseshoe magnet. She held it towards the medal. Alfred felt the pull, as the medal snapped to the magnet. She nodded. 'And put your socks or something on inside out. That should do it.'

After he got dressed, he packed his swimming stuff and ate breakfast. Granny drank tea while she collected the last bits she needed for the market. He helped her carry the big woven tote bags to her car—an old sky-blue VW Beetle.

'Try not to upset the little people and remember to lock the door,' she said before getting into her car. Then she rolled the window down and called, 'Have fun at the lake!'

Alfred waved at her, thinking how much more relaxed she seemed, now that she knew he had the sight. Perhaps that was the only reason she hadn't wanted him to stay with her.

Back inside, he walked from room to room, from one woodcarving to the next. He didn't touch them. He just stared and wondered how they might be protecting the cottage.

In addition to the water sprite and the face with the forked tongue, there was a mole, a bat, a bear, a catfish and an eagle. The two small figurines were faerie creatures. The five cat-sized carvings were all animals, but what did those animals have in common?

Three were mammals. Two could fly. One lived under water. A real bear was much bigger than the other animals, though the carvings were the same size.

He thought back to the first things he'd noticed about each of them. The bear's snout. The bat's ears. The eagle's eyes.

Eagle eyes. That's what you said about someone who was sharp-sighted. And the eagle kept watch from the front room window. Everyone knew bats had excellent hearing. And a bear could sniff out food from miles away. So if the carvings were keeping watch with their predominant senses, those three covered sight, hearing and smell. Moles were almost blind, but wasn't there something about their sense of touch being acute? That left taste. Were fish good at tasting? Perhaps. He'd have to look that up.

The wooden creatures might be a kind of sensory alarm system, but that still didn't explain how they protected anything or anyone. Or why they so often appeared in his nightmares.

He had a feeling the fork-tongued figurine played a more active role. After all, hadn't Mr Tumbleweed, who was a faerie creature, had his worst fit after seeing it above the front door.

And then there was the water sprite...

Alfred hesitated, before he pushed the door to Granny's bedroom open. Even though she wasn't at home, he tiptoed round her bed. Squatting by her bedside table, he pushed the lamp to the side, so he could study the little figurine. He wasn't going to touch her and fall under her spell.

But the way she smiled her sad smile at him... The way her long hair flowed in soft curls... He couldn't resist.

First he just caressed her hair with one finger. Letting out a deep breath, a tight knot in his belly unravelled. Then he grasped the figurine and cradled her against his chest, and it was as if his whole body sighed in relief.

Outside, a bicycle bell dinged, and Saga called his name.

He wanted to put the figurine back, he really did. But he just couldn't.

Before he could regret taking it, he was on the front step, locking the door, stuffing the little water sprite into his trouser pocket. He walked down the garden path, without a backwards glance at the other woodcarvings.

12

Underwater Song

The lake was so big it could've been the sea. Beyond the far shore, green hills reached for the puffy clouds. Boats spread out over the water, their triangular sails like arrows.

After Alfred and Saga had locked their bikes among rows of bicycles by a kiosk, Mr Tumbleweed jumped out of the basket and into a gorse bush.

'He doesn't like being near this many people,' Saga said, as they walked onto a crowded grass embankment with a patchwork of towels. 'At school, he always waits outside.'

Alfred wished he could hide in the gorse too.

The last two metres before the water was a narrow sandy strip full of stones. He dreaded having to cross it in his bare feet, until he noticed that almost everyone wore some kind of water shoes. They kept them on when they went swimming. His trainers could survive getting wet. Perhaps no one would notice he was different.

As soon as they'd put their towels down, Saga took a stack of slightly crumpled paper out of her shoulder bag. *Stop the tunnel project* was written in bold red marker above *Join the protest on Friday, 4 August at 10 a.m.*

They were actually doing this. He was part of arranging a protest against Dad's work project. How would Dad react if he found out?

'Our printer didn't work. My hand's so sore,' she said, when she caught him staring. 'Do you want to go together or split up?'

'Together.'

They started walking from towel to towel, from parents with small children, to elderly couples, to groups of teenagers or kids their own age. Saga talked about the pond and biodiversity and protecting nature. She didn't mention faeries. Her passion was unwavering, no matter if the parents hardly listened, the old people called her sweet or the other kids sniggered and muttered she was weird.

Alfred wished he could've turned invisible, but he tried his best to get people to accept the homemade flyers. Few promised to come.

They had almost reached the end of the grass embankment when Saga hesitated. Only one group of kids remained. In front of where they were sitting, a jetty jutted out into the water.

'It's no use talking to them,' she muttered, tapping the bridge of her glasses. 'They're in my year.'

Alfred glanced at the group.

'What are you looking at?' one of them—a boy—yelled.

'Who's your friend, weirdo?' another boy shouted.

'Did you finally kiss that toad, Saga?' a girl called.

'Too bad it didn't turn into a prince,' the first boy added. 'Or is that your fairy prince?'

They all guffawed.

'Good one.' The two boys high-fived.

'You know what... We are going to talk to them.' Saga's face split in a wide smile. 'Are you really as good at swimming as your granny says?'

Alfred shrugged. 'Probably.'

Resolutely, Saga strode over to the group with Alfred in tow. What was she up to now? He had a feeling he wouldn't like it, but there was no stopping her.

'He might not be a prince,' she said. 'But he's a swimming star.'

The two boys and a couple of the girls, including the one who'd spoken, stared at Alfred's shoulders under the red T-shirt, trying to gauge his muscles. Some of them sniggered.

'Oh, I forgot. You think you're pretty fast in the water, don't you?' Saga said.

'Pretty fast! Kev came first in the school championships. I was second,' the first boy said.

'I bet you Alfred is faster.'

'Alfred,' Kev said in a singsong mocking tone. 'That's your boyfriend's name?'

'What's the bet?' the other boy asked. They both looked tanned and fit. When they got to their feet, they were half a head taller than Alfred.

'If Alfred wins, you all have to come to the protest tomorrow. If you win, you can have my babysitting money to buy ice cream.' Saga flashed a banknote. Alfred saw the number twenty in a corner. 'And there's the honour, of course.'

'What are you doing?' Alfred hissed. 'I don't...' He wanted to say that he didn't wish to swim in the lake at all. Not like this. He'd only planned on splashing a bit with his head above water. The last time he'd been swimming in water that wasn't surrounded by concrete was two years ago on a beach holiday.

When he'd ducked under the surface, the water—its music and beauty and taste—had dazzled him. The unparalleled feeling of freedom had made him want to swim to the end of the world. It had been both wonderful and terrifying.

'Hours of sweating in the sun at your lame protest against a measly ice cream.' Kev shook his head. 'Not worth it. Unless... On top of ice cream... We want to see you kiss your toad.'

Sniggers and giggles erupted from the group.

'Good one!' The other boy said and they high-fived again.

Saga frowned. Her eyes roamed behind the groups where the gorse grew. Alfred tried to spot the tree sprite too. She whispered, 'Okay.'

From one of the nearest bushes, Alfred heard the familiar groaning voice, 'Kiss! Somebody is agreeing to kiss this one body, who has very nearly had enough. Somebody is close to the last twig. One more drop and the cup—'

'From the jetty to that buoy and back.' Kev pointed. 'That's about 400 metres, right, Patrick?'

Patrick nodded. 'Freestyle. And we win if one of us beats him.'

Saga, of course, hadn't heard Mr Tumbleweed. In her whirlwind fashion, she'd made promises on behalf of both Alfred and the tree sprite. He looked from the jetty along the shore to the orange mooring buoy that bobbed on the surface. It wasn't far. And there didn't seem to be any way of getting out of the bet. He nodded.

'Deal,' she said.

They all shook hands.

Saga ran back to their towels to get their stuff, saying Alfred should just prepare mentally. He went out to the end of the jetty and took off his T-shirt and the shorts he wore over his swimming trunks. Kev had told him the water was deep enough for a dive start, so he pulled off his shoes and inside-out socks too. Then he sat down on the splintered wood until Saga arrived with his goggles.

He leant on his longest leg, while Saga and another girl counted down from three.

At 'go,' he dived.

The cool, fresh water shocked his body awake. The lake was nothing like a pool. Everything was alive. Small fish darted between the swaying green seagrass. Shellfish scuttled behind stones. Tiny sediments floated around him, catching sun rays.

His head filled with joyous music. Every stream and river that ran into the lake made its own unique tinkling sounds. He wanted to listen to all of them.

A swirl in the water made the sediments spiral. It came from a foot. From one of the other swimmers.

The race! He had to concentrate on the race.

Alfred tore himself away and came up from the dive. The others were already in front of him. Swimming towards the buoy, he closed his eyes when his face was under water. To avoid the distracting music, he counted a rhythm in his head.

Before they reached the buoy, he overtook both boys. On the return stretch, the distance to them grew. His hands ploughed through the water. His feet flexed and stretched in rapid drumbeats. It felt so good, so natural, he forgot to count.

The music poured in through his ears. There were voices too. A distant choir sang. Most of the words were unclear, but he thought he heard his mother's name. He stopped moving his arms so he could hear better. There it was again. Nereida.

There were too many other sounds near the surface. Someone yelling, 'Swim,' splashing, a dog barking. Alfred let himself sink down onto the soft seagrass. All he wanted was to hear his mother's name again. Nothing else mattered.

It wasn't until two shadows darkened the lake floor that he remembered the race. He shot up to the surface, but by then it was too late. Ahead of him, both boys reached the jetty.

'What happened?' Saga asked. 'Are you okay?'

'He let us win, that's what happened.' Kev shook his head.

'Weirdo,' Patrick muttered as he climbed the ladder.

While Saga handed over her money and explained that she didn't know where her toad was, Alfred stayed under the jetty, treading water. He hadn't managed to blend in. They had all noticed he was different. And he'd failed Saga. At the one thing he was actually good at, he'd failed.

'Next time we see you, you'd better kiss it.'

'At the protest tomorrow?' Saga's voice was unnaturally bright.

'As if we'd come to your stupid protest.'

After the others left, she climbed down into the water.

'I'm sorry. I don't know... I just couldn't...' Alfred said. 'Dad gave me pocket money. I'll pay you.'

'I don't care about the money. I just want a crowd for the protest tomorrow. And it's not your fault you couldn't beat them.' Her forehead puckered above her glasses. 'Or needed a breather or whatever.'

But it was his fault. He could've easily beaten them. If only he hadn't heard his mother's name.

'It doesn't matter. They probably wouldn't have come anyway.' Saga climbed out. 'Let's just go.'

After drying himself, Alfred pulled his shorts on over his damp swimming trunks, taking care that the little water sprite didn't fall out of the pocket.

'What about the market? Could we hand out flyers there?' he asked, when they reached the bicycles, wishing he could make up for botching the race.

'Your granny's doing that.' Saga whistled for Mr Tumbleweed.

The strange creature trudged out from behind a bush, wagging the broken twig Saga had bandaged. He grumbled about having had enough of humans making promises and somebody losing on purpose and a twig for a twig.

Saga obviously couldn't hear him, because she just waited for him to jump into the basket.

A chill ran up Alfred's back. Giving Saga the money wouldn't appease the tree sprite. He didn't know what would, and he really didn't want to deal with one more vindictive faerie.

 13

The Faerie in the Forest

They cycled back uphill without talking. The helmet felt tight on Alfred's head, as if his hair had expanded after getting wet. He tried to recall the music from the lake, the way the choir had sung 'Nereida'. Saga trod on the pedals and pulled ahead.

When they reached the lane that ran past the farm and the chapel to Granny's cottage, the forest loomed over them. Only a narrow strip of long grass with wildflowers separated it from the asphalt. A trail led in under the shadow of the branches.

'Wait,' he called, getting off his bike.

Saga made a half-circle and freewheeled back to him.

'What? Did the chain jump off?'

Alfred shook his head, then hurried to speak before he could change his mind. 'Do you really believe there's a way into Faerie from one of the sinkholes? Can you show me one of them? I've never seen a sinkhole.'

Saga looked at her watch. 'Yes and yes. I have to be home soon, but I can show you the nearest one. Why d'you ask?'

'Because...' He hesitated and stuck his hand in his pocket to touch the water-sprite figurine for courage. It was a long time since he had trusted anyone with his innermost thoughts—Dad didn't even know about the incident after the last swimming competition. But he felt he could trust Saga. Trust her not to think he was weird.

'Because,' he said again. 'I don't think my mother's dead.'

It didn't take Alfred long to tell Saga what he knew about his mother's empty grave. There had always been rumours about disappearances in the woods, Saga told him. Nereida wasn't the first to vanish without a trace. Some people were found, like the two engineers, without any memories of the time they'd been gone, but others never returned.

'That's one reason people in the olden days started calling it the Faerie Hill,' Saga said. 'Most locals still call it that, even if they don't actually believe in faeries.'

Alfred hesitated. Granny believed in faeries, and she'd asked him to stay away from the forest. After his mother's disappearance, perhaps she was right to be worried.

'Is it dangerous?' He pointed up at the trees.

'Nah... I go hiking in the woods all the time. As long as you're protected.' She waved a hand at his red T-shirt and inside-out socks.

Mr Tumbleweed growled something indistinct, as he bounded out of sight.

'We just need a name for you.' Saga locked their bicycles together, and they began walking towards the trees.

'Why?'

'We can't risk that the faeries hear your real name. What do you think of Nemo? I always wanted to use that. It means 'nobody' in Latin and that could be handy if they ask "Who's there?"' She spoke the question in a squeaky voice.

'Okay.' Alfred thought it was a very fitting name for himself. 'What should I call you?'

'Saga.' She stopped and looked back at him with a frown. 'Did you think that's my real name?'

Alfred shrugged. 'So, what is your real name?'

'I'm not telling anyone. Ever. I've used Saga for so long, I don't think my parents even remember what they named me.'

Underneath the trees, they followed a narrow path uphill. Saga stopped to pick up litter. She showed him a discarded chocolate wrapper before she put it in a small pouch that hung from her belt.

'That's another thing the faeries don't like. Can you believe people just leave their rubbish behind? It pollutes the streams and the rivers. I bet you the water sprites hate when something like this gets tangled in their hair.'

Alfred's scalp prickled at the thought. The tingle moved down to the back of his neck. He had a feeling of being watched, but there was no one nearby. No one that he could see.

'There's a small sinkhole right over here.' Saga took a few steps away from the path, before she got down on hands and knees. 'It's tricky to see.'

Crawling, Alfred followed her until they came to the rim of a hole in the ground. Across, it wasn't much bigger than an inflatable paddling pool. Tree roots latticed one wall. Another sloped, covered by moss, like a green slide into the darkness below. They lay next to each other and looked into the sinkhole. Its depth was impossible to guess.

Alfred felt a tug deep in his stomach. 'What's down there?'

'Caves. Tunnels. I don't know. On the other side of the hill, there are some dripstone caves that are open to the public. We went on an excursion with my class once. It's the reason the motorway tunnel is going through this side. They want to conserve that area.'

'But what if there are caves on this side that are worth protecting?'

'Then they haven't been discovered.'

Behind them, Mr Tumbleweed emitted a strange high-pitched croak. They half-turned. He was trembling so much his twiggy fingers rattled and the bandage on his broken twig unspooled.

'Faeries!' Saga shoved herself away from the rim, but she pushed too hard. The ground under Alfred's hand gave way. A lump of chalky rock with grass hair tumbled down into the hole. Alfred landed on his elbow before scrambling back.

The rock hit the underground bottom with a dull, echoing thump.

A musical voice said, 'Careful now.'

When Alfred looked up, an extraordinarily tall woman had appeared beyond the sinkhole. She wore a floor-length green dress that blended into the mossy ground and a necklace of large shimmering black beads that seemed to be moving. Her long silvery hair was spotted like birch bark and plaited and fastened with butterfly hair clips. Leaves and flickering sunlight danced over her translucent skin. Alfred couldn't tell if she was young or old. She definitely wasn't human.

'Is something wrong with that... creature?' the woman asked. She came closer to him, walking right by the edge of the sinkhole without even looking at the ground.

Alfred tore his eyes away from her to glance over his shoulder at Saga. Mr Tumbleweed threw himself down on the path. His little stick arms flew to his face, and it looked like he was trying to cover both his eyes and his ears with his small hands while he tossed around in the dirt. Saga tried to pin him down, mumbling calming words.

'The likeness is astounding,' the woman said.

Alfred's head swirled back. She wasn't looking at Mr Tumbleweed, but gazed at him with eyes so dark they were like bottomless sinkholes.

'Are you talking about me? My mother?'

'What did you say?' Saga called.

Alfred ignored her. It was as if Saga were calling to him from far away. Her struggle to calm Mr Tumbleweed didn't concern him.

The woman didn't even look in Saga's direction. 'There is no doubt you are your mother's child.' She smiled at Alfred.

'Do you know where she is?'

'Nemo!'

It took a moment for Alfred to realize Saga meant him.

'I like your name... Nemo,' the woman said with a slight hesitation, as if she knew it wasn't his real name. 'You can call me Amanita. Why don't you come with me?'

One of the black beads on the woman's necklace spread its wings and took off. It was some kind of beetle. With arms. Thin black arms that it was waving in the air, shooing Alfred away. But it didn't get far. The woman twirled one hand in a graceful motion, and the beetle fell to the ground. The other beetles scuttled closer together to fill the gap in her necklace.

'Can you take me to my mother?'

Amanita held out a slim, pale hand, saying, 'Let us find her together.'

'Nemo! Stop!' Saga yelled.

Before he could step closer towards Amanita, a bird with an enormous wingspan swooped down between them and made straight for his head. Two yellow eyes scowled at him. An orange beak opened wide and screeched. He ducked, hiding his face in his hands. After the swoosh of a single wingbeat, a wave of air swept down over him.

The bird screamed again.

Still crouching, Alfred saw it glide away between tall trees.

'Was that an eagle?' he asked Amanita while he got up, but she didn't answer.

Amanita had vanished.

He squinted, trying to spot her, calling, 'Amanita! Come back. Amanita!'

Further uphill, he thought he saw a particular stretch of mossy ground flutter.

'Where did she go?' he called to Saga. 'Why did you have to interrupt?'

The little creature in her arms had calmed down.

'Did you just talk to a faerie? I've never seen him have such a bad reaction. Except at your granny's house.'

'You mean you couldn't see her?'

'Of course I couldn't see her. But I heard how you were about to go with her.'

'She wanted to help me find my mother,' he said in a choked voice. 'She's a real faerie and she knows my mother! It's proof, isn't it? Proof that my mother disappeared into the faerie realm, that she's still there...'

Perhaps she was trapped in that eternal dance Saga had mentioned, or under an enchantment that had made her forget her family. There were endless possibilities of what could've happened to his mother in that other world. Best of all, those possibilities had absolutely nothing to do with him.

A bubble of hope swelled in Alfred's chest.

14

A Snip of Scissors

For a long while, Alfred didn't speak. The bubble of hope felt fragile. It might burst if he said the wrong thing. If Saga said the wrong thing. He just wanted to imagine his mother safe and well in an enchanted garden she couldn't escape.

Saga checked the time on her watch and groaned. 'I'm so late. Mum's going to be livid if I'm not home when the girls get back.'

'Where do you think the entrance to the faerie realm is?' Alfred asked.

'At the biggest sinkhole,' she answered without hesitation.

'Why?'

'It's different. You'll understand when you see it.'

'Is it up there?' He pointed in the direction Amanita had disappeared.

Saga nodded.

'Can I find it myself?'

'No, that's too dangerous. You don't know the woods. Come on.' Saga started down the path. 'I'll show you tomorrow, after the protest. Tell me about the faerie.'

Perhaps he could stay and call for Amanita. She might appear if he was on his own. Or she might not, and he would be completely lost.

He half-ran to catch up, keeping his eyes on the ground to avoid stumbling. He tried to describe Amanita's appearance, but it was as if the details weren't fixed. Her hair which he thought had been whitish, could just as easily have been black. He couldn't recall the shape of her features. Only her black bottomless eyes and the beetle necklace were clear in his mind.

'Did you see the eagle?' he asked.

'Of course. It was enormous.'

'I think I saw it when we cycled to the tunnel site yesterday too.'

'What? The same one?'

He could hear how unlikely it was that he should have recognized it. 'Maybe not.'

'What's really strange is that the faerie said her name was Amanita. That she would tell you her name, I mean. Names have power. And Amanita... I think I have heard it before somewhere.'

'She said to call her Amanita. Not that it was her actual name. And I think she knew Nemo wasn't my real name.'

They walked the rest of the way to their bicycles in silence.

At the cottage, Alfred first inspected the garden. Everything outside the bolted shed seemed to be in order, but the ceramic dish under the rose hedge was licked clean. He hurried inside to fetch more milk. Perhaps if he got on good terms with the little people, they could help him find the way to the faerie realm.

While he crouched by the bushes and refilled the dish, he stared in between the leaves and thorns.

'I'm sorry, okay? I didn't mean to hit you with the stick,' he said. 'Can we talk? I brought fresh milk. Please don't run away.'

At first, there was no answer, then the little people chatted as if he couldn't hear them.

'What's he saying, Little Mother?'

'He says, he's sorry, and he wants us so fat on milk we can't run away.'

'That's not true. I just—'

'He will be sorry, I'm sure. He will be ever so sorry if She lets us have the scissors.'

'Who? What scissors?' he asked, fearing further harm to Granny's flowers or yarn.

'We haven't had the scissors in so long. Oh, Little Father, I hope we get the scissors.'

'Do you want to borrow scissors? Or can I get you something else to drink?' Alfred asked.

'Tell him what we want, Little Mother.'

'A winter that's mild, a world returned to wild, and we'll happily take your firstborn child,' Little Mother chanted.

Little Father chuckled. 'I long to hear the snip, snip, snip of the scissors, Little Mother.'

'And the snap too, Little Father. Let's go now. The shadow snap is the sweetest sound...' The voices became indistinct as the little people scuttled away.

Alfred got to his feet and trudged back into the cottage. Had he just made everything worse?

After a dinner of sourdough bread, honey-baked ham and soft cheese Granny had bought at the market, they sat in her front room. The heap of tangled yarn lay on the table between them. She instructed Alfred, as they began to pull the threads apart.

Winding yellow yarn into a ball, Alfred asked, 'What will Dad say to us being at the protest tomorrow? Saga told me you're involved too.'

'Well, he knows I've been against the tunnel from the outset. And as for you, dear...' Granny pulled a green ball through a tangle. 'You're your own person. Look at Saga. It's only right that you, young people, stand up for your beliefs. Your father had just learned to walk when I took him along to his first protest march... He'll understand.'

For a moment she sat with a faraway look in her eyes, until Alfred cleared his throat and pointed at his thread, which was stuck in a gigantic knot.

'Let me just snip that,' Granny said, smiling.

Her smile vanished when Alfred told her about his encounter with Little Mother and Little Father and those scissors they wanted to snip and snap.

'Why do you stay here, when the little people are terrorizing you?'

Granny handed him the end of a turquoise thread. 'First of all, living so close to the faeries is not all bad. I wouldn't be able to get my colours without the spring, without its glamour.'

On the table, the bright threads seemed to flow together like an actual stream. Alfred blinked and tugged at a loose knot.

He wanted to ask about Amanita, without having to tell Granny he'd been in the forest. 'Are there other faeries here?'

'Many, I'm sure. But they are troublesome things. I don't go looking for them, and I stay away from the woods.'

'You never go into the forest?'

'Not these past twelve years. You shouldn't either.'

Before Granny could extract any kind of promise from him, Alfred said, 'You said, "first of all", when I asked why you stay.'

'Well, secondly, the cottage is my home. I grew up here. My granny minded me while my parents worked. I helped her in the garden... put milk out for the urchins. That's what she used to call the little people. It's an old name for hedgehogs. I suppose they are keeping me here too—all my memories.'

Alfred wondered if memories were the reason Dad was running away from the place. Would they have stayed if his mother hadn't disappeared?

'After my granny died, my grandfather gave me the cottage. Neither he nor my mother had the sight, so he didn't want to remain here. It's easy to upset the little people when you can see them. It's impossible not to cross them when you can't.'

'What about my mother? Did she have the sight?' He couldn't see Granny's eyes, but looked at his own reflection in her reading glasses.

'Oh, Alfred...' The worry-wrinkles formed choppy waves on her forehead. 'Oh no, look at this knot.' She bent low over the yarn heap.

'Did she have the sight, Granny?'

Without looking up, Granny muttered, 'She could see all the faeries. And, unfortunately, she loved the woods.' She cut the threads of a big, tangled knot, saying, 'Those nasty critters have really done it this time... I think we'll save the rest for tomorrow. Time for bed.'

Before Alfred could ask any more questions, she started turning off lamps.

As he left the dark front room, he looked back at the carved creatures. Most of the catfish was hidden behind the armchair.

But the cone of light from the hallway lit up the eagle's wings. He willed them to move. They didn't.

He'd been sitting with his back to the eagle all night. Now he wished he'd studied its piercing eyes. Were they not exactly like the real eagle's eyes?

Once again, he wondered what the link was between the cottage and the woodcarvings.

His mother's carvings. Could they have come from the faerie realm?

It was only when he got undressed that he realized the little water-sprite figurine was still in his pocket. It was too late to return her to Granny's room, and he fell asleep stroking her hair, dreaming, again, of swimming in the forest river.

The Protest Leader

When Granny and Alfred arrived at the farm the next morning, the kitchen was already full of people drinking tea or coffee and getting ready to march. It was even more chaotic than the first time Alfred visited.

'Hi, Alfred! Can you believe Florian and Oliver aren't coming?' Saga said, as if he knew who they were, before she disappeared in the crowd.

'Good to see you, Alfred,' her mum said. She handed him a glass of elderflower cordial and ruffled his hair. He normally hated it when people did that, but with her he didn't mind.

Saga's uncle, a large man with a huge beard in cut-off jeans and sandals, banged two pot lids together, and people quieted down. Alfred expected him to start speaking. Instead, Saga climbed up on the kitchen counter.

'Thanks for coming, everyone,' she began. 'This might be our last chance to stop the people that want to ruin our nature with that tunnel. The insects and the birds and the otters can't stop them. The trees can't stop them. Not even the Faerie Hill itself, and whatever lives inside it, can stop them.

We have to do that. We have to make them see that nature is worth more than a motorway tunnel. We must stop them. We can stop them!'

The room erupted in cheers and clapping. Alfred clapped as hard as anyone. Saga's Faerie Investigation Society might be a one-woman show, but this was big. And Saga was the leader.

Before they set off, everyone carried the big placards outside and got ready to march. Alfred tried to get Saga's mum on his own in the kitchen, but Poppy and Daisy were there too, running around, playing with the cat. Mr Tumbleweed grumbled at them whenever he had to jump out of their way.

After marching through the village and along the country lanes, they met up with other protesters by the track to the building site. A sizeable crowd appeared to have gathered. But there weren't more than maybe a hundred people. None of the kids from the lake had come. Why didn't any of them care about nature?

Now, they stood at the edge of the huge gravel plane with its heavy machinery, like a small colony of ants waiting to be squashed.

Alfred heard mutters around him about friends and relatives who'd said they wanted to come but couldn't. They'd had to go to work or look after children or do the weekly shop.

'Why don't they understand that we must act now, or it'll be too late?' Saga hissed.

Her uncle placed a hand on her shoulder and said, 'They don't believe they have time for disruption in their daily lives. They don't realize what's at stake, Saga.'

Did Dad realize what was at stake, Alfred wondered. Did he know that the Faerie Hill might hide the clues to his mother's disappearance?

A honk sounded behind them. Several black cars and a van from the local news station idled on the gravel road. The protesters raised their placards and blocked the cars from entering the building site. They began chanting, 'Protect nature! Save our wildlife! No drill into the Faerie Hill! Protect nature! Save our wildlife! No drill into the Faerie Hill...'

More vehicles arrived, including three police cars. The procession of cars inched forward, trying to force the protesters to the side.

Saga raised one hand, silencing everyone, and shouted, 'Sit down!'

As one, the crowd sat on the gravel road. Alfred was right behind Saga, looking up at the first car. Heat from its engine pulsed towards them. A reporter and a cameraman came running from the news van. Police officers marched up alongside the cars. The protesters started chanting again.

Unfortunately, with the help of the building-site workers, it wasn't long until the police had split the group.

In a mostly peaceful manner, people moved out of the way. Alfred too. Saga was the last person sitting in the middle of the road, and she had to be dragged to the side by a burly police officer. The cameraman filmed as everyone was cordoned off at the sides of the track.

Alfred stayed by Saga and her uncle. Granny was on the other side, chanting as loudly as everyone else when the cars passed between them.

After the cars parked by the office containers, people in suits emerged from them. Dad was there too. He'd thrown a blazer over his khaki work trousers, and he wore a hard hat and heavy shoes. He looked like he was caught in the middle between the officials in their suits and the workers. For once, it looked like he didn't belong.

Despite what Granny had said, Alfred took a step to the side, so he was hidden behind Saga's uncle. He wanted to tell Dad to save the Faerie Hill, but he couldn't do so in front of a crowd.

Saga was banging the stick of her placard into the ground and shouting the chant, with the TV camera just in front of her.

'Silence for Mayor Underwood!' A tinny voice called through a megaphone.

The chanting continued.

A portly little man in a dark grey suit grabbed the megaphone.

'Welcome!' The mayor boomed, his bushy moustache spread above a wide smile. 'It's wonderful to see so many enthusiastic voters have braved the heat,' he continued, as if he hadn't read the placards and couldn't hear the chants, which now turned to boos.

The other officials clapped politely. No one else appeared to be in favour of the tunnel. A woman in a skirt and jacket, next to the mayor, fanned herself with a binder.

'Today is a great day—groundbreaking, you might say.' The mayor waved a hand behind him, where three diggers stood lined up, tied together with red ribbon. Three workers stood by the machines, ready to drive them to the hill.

The mayor waffled on for a while, talking about the importance of the motorway and sounding as full of himself as he had on the radio. Alfred couldn't hear much for all the booing. When the mayor finished speaking, an assistant handed him and the woman in the skirt, who apparently was from the regional planning commission, a pair of scissors each.

The two officials walked together to the ribbons, and after a nod from the mayor, cut them at the same time. The engines of the three yellow diggers fired up. With their trowels raised high in the air, pointing downwards, they began to roll slowly across the flattened surface towards the steep cliff.

'Come on,' Saga yelled. She ducked under the arms of the burly police officer. He made a grab for her, managing to grip the strap of her shoulder bag. She shrugged out of it and slipped away, leaving him holding her bag.

Stunned, Alfred stood frozen to the spot. She'd asked him to come. But he couldn't run in front of all these people.

'Run, Saga!' her uncle called, as she raced to catch up with the diggers.

Alfred stilled his breath, stilled his heart, hiding himself, and made his way back through the rows of people. He scrambled up on the hillock where they had stood two days earlier.

When he looked back down, Saga was between the diggers. Two police officers were striding into the cloud of dust after them. The cameraman and the journalist followed close behind.

Saga rounded the middle of the diggers and threw herself down in front of it. The heavy machines ground to a halt.

'No drill into the Faerie Hill!' she yelled.

The other protesters began chanting, 'Protect nature! Save our wildlife! No drill into the Faerie Hill!'

But it was no use.

Although Saga thrashed and flailed her arms, much like Alfred had seen Mr Tumbleweed do, the police officers and two workers each grabbed hold of one of her limbs and carried her towards the container office.

What could he do? He touched the water-sprite figurine in his pocket.

'Mr Tumbleweed,' he called, hoping the tree sprite could somehow help Saga. But the creature didn't appear.

The machines fired up again. With loud grinding noises, the three diggers slammed their trowels down into the hillside. Large chunks of the cliff tumbled to the ground.

Dad and Saga's uncle both hurried towards the office.

'The tunnel project has officially begun.' The mayor's voice boomed through the megaphone. 'On Monday, the unstoppable tunnel boring machine will arrive and start drilling.'

Alfred had seen those tunnel boring machines on other building sites. 'Moles', Dad called them. Like moles, they bored their way through the underground. Unlike moles, they could make their way through the hardest materials, their rotating cutter discs slicing and grinding rock into dust.

A few officials clapped. Some protesters turned around and trudged down the road, Granny among them. She had skipped the market for the protest and knew Alfred was planning to spend the rest of the day with Saga. The remaining protesters waited, lost and downcast.

Alfred was watching the diggers scrape the hill into a vertical wall, when he heard familiar voices from somewhere under the nearest thorn bush.

'The tree sprite's girl is their leader, Little Father.'

'I saw, Little Mother. With my own eyes, I saw how she directed them.'

Alfred nodded to himself. For once, the little people had got something right. Saga was a true leader, and he couldn't believe how brave she was.

'She led them right to our hill,' Little Mother said.

'She showed those yellow monsters where to dig.'

'She'll be sorry, when we get the scissors!'

'No! That's not true.' Alfred got down on all fours by the bush. 'She ran in front of the yellow monsters to try to stop them. Didn't you see?'

'Don't believe a word that one says, Little Father. He wants to fatten us on milk.'

'I don't,' Alfred said. 'Please listen to me!'

'They'll both be sorry,' Little Father said as the creatures scuttled away.

'Wait,' he called, chasing after them. 'She tried to stop them!'

Near the path up to the forest, their green hat and chequered scarf popped up between the wildflowers a few times, but the pixies were too nimble and well-camouflaged.

'All the humans will be sorry,' Little Mother screeched, before Alfred lost sight of them completely.

As he walked back downhill, he wondered what they were planning.

16

The Spy in the Sinkhole

Alfred stood on the hillock and watched the cars drive away. The grinding noise from the diggers drowned out all other sounds.

When Dad came out of the office, Alfred waved, but Dad didn't look his way. He turned towards the cliff face behind the diggers, raised his head and stared up at the forest. Someone tapped Dad on the shoulder and spoke to him, before he got into one of the black cars.

A short while later, Saga and her uncle followed a police officer towards the last police car. Alfred wondered if she had been arrested. But the officer just wagged a finger at Saga, shook her uncle's hand and left.

On her way to the remaining protesters, Saga glanced around and saw Alfred. She hugged her uncle before she climbed the hillock. As she reached Alfred, Mr Tumbleweed bounced out from behind a bush further downhill. He had two of his twiggy fingers in his ears.

'I don't know what to do,' Saga said and sank down in the high grass, turning her back to the building site, with her face in her hands. 'People just don't get it. They don't understand that we can't continue to destroy nature. Even that policeman—my uncle went to school with him—he doesn't think they should build the tunnel either, but all he talked about was having to do his job...'

'And my dad is part of it.' Alfred sat down next to her. What was Dad thinking?

Below them, the idyllic pond glimmered in shifting patterns of sunlight and shade. Soon it would be gone. The stream wasn't far away, but he couldn't hear its music for the noise of the diggers. And it wasn't only the pond that would disappear. What if the drill ruined the entry to Faerie or the realm itself?

'You were really brave,' he said. He'd have to be brave too. If they couldn't stop the tunnel, he'd have to find a way to Faerie and find his mother, before she was lost for ever.

'It didn't slow them down for more than five minutes, did it? On Monday when that tunnel-thingy comes, it will all be too late.'

'Can you still show me that sinkhole?'

Sighing, Saga got to her feet. 'Yeah, okay.'

At first, the forest was full of light and life. In the airy space between trees, smaller plants grew lush and untamed. Insects buzzed around them, inaudible below the din from the building site. Brambles dotted with unripe pink berries and white flowers crept across the path, so Alfred had to watch his steps.

As they continued up the hill, the trees grew closer together. They blocked the sunlight. The path became steeper. And rockier. It wound round roots that stuck out of the earth. Thick carpets of bright green moss covered the shadows and ate their way up north-facing sides of white rocks and tree trunks. The noise from the building site became a low growl.

When he wasn't looking at the ground, Alfred peered around, trying to spot the little people or other faeries. Saga didn't pause at any of the forks in the path or when she ducked under branches onto even more overgrown trails. Mr Tumbleweed sprang ahead, jumping from rock to rock.

'How do you know which path to take? This place is like a labyrinth.' To rest a moment, Alfred took his phone out and looked at the map, but the screen was completely white with a couple of thin grey roads at the bottom. Like at Granny's cottage, he had neither data nor phone reception.

'This is nothing compared to what it must be like underneath, in the tunnels,' Saga called. 'There's even supposed to be an underground river.'

The path became steeper for a while, although Alfred hadn't thought that was possible, until at last the ground plateaued.

Through the trees, he saw one of the cone-like hills that Dad had told him was an extinct volcano. Their trail continued right up to where the almost vertical cliff rose in front of them. As they came nearer, Alfred could make out the crumbling remnants of a wall at the very top of the cone.

'What's up there?' He leant his head back.

'An old fort. The ruins of a fort. There used to be a trail... See where a rockfall has taken it away?' Saga pointed to a place about halfway up the cliff. 'Now you need climbing gear to ascend.'

Alfred saw a thin line cross the bare rock—a steel wire glinting in the sun.

'We're going the other way. It's almost flat from here on.' Saga and Mr Tumbleweed strode ahead for a while, before she called, 'It's right over here.'

When Alfred caught up, she pointed to a sign with *DANGER* and 30M *DROP* in bold capital letters above an image of a stick figure falling down a cliff.

A wooden fence stood on one side of the sign and encircled most of the sinkhole. But on the other side of the sign, the fence lay flat on the ground, covered by ivy-like creepers.

'That's strange,' Saga said, as they walked closer to the sinkhole. 'That fence was standing last week. And look at it now.'

Alfred wondered if the fence had been there twelve years ago.

Saga stepped closer, squatted down, and reached for the ivy-covered fence post.

'Don't touch that!' Alfred yelled. 'It's poison ivy!'

'We don't have poison ivy here.' She pinched a leaf between thumb and forefinger.

'See the three leaflets...' Alfred's voice trailed off, before he could explain how you recognized poison ivy.

The leaves were oddly pale, and they had just moved. All of them. Not the way leaves swayed in the wind. Every single leaf moved at once and in the same direction.

'Ouch!' Saga held her hand towards him so he could see the red rash on the tips of her fingers.

Alfred squatted and leant over a vine. Like poison ivy, the leaves were in sets of three. But their pale silvery shine looked unnatural. And the purple veins on them pulsated every time the vines moved, as if they were living creatures.

'Look at the fence!' Saga said, just as the vines and all the leaves took another jerk forward. Purposefully and coordinated, they pushed ahead, like an advancing army.

The fallen fence moved too. The creepers had wound themselves round its top horizontal bar and they were dragging it over the undergrowth. The fence posts had broken off near the ground, the splintering tops sticking out of the ivy.

'Do you think the plants did this?' Alfred stepped round to the other side of the sign. From here, he could see how the ivy-like vines climbed up the far side of the limestone wall and out of the sinkhole.

Holding onto the fence, he looked down, and then he understood why Saga thought this sinkhole was different.

The hole, which was four or five metres across, was merely a small opening in the domed ceiling of an enormous cave. A mist of cooler, muggy air hung just below the surface. At the bottom of the cave—thirty metres below, according to the sign—moss and the strange creepers covered the ground. Here and there, rocks and crooked trees poked out of the green carpet. It was almost as if the sinkhole itself were a different world. And with those peculiar plants...

Alfred's heart pounded. This had to be a way into the faerie realm.

'Is this the entrance, Mr Tumbleweed?' he asked, but the tree sprite didn't answer.

'It looks like the plants might be heading down where we came from.' Saga had come to stand next to him.

'What if... You said the other day that faeries care about nature... And that they wouldn't want anyone to drill into the hill. What if they could help stop the tunnel?'

A smile spread across Saga's face. 'You're a genius! I never thought of that before, because I couldn't see or talk to the faeries. But now I can—through you, I can. So we need to find a faerie—perhaps the one you talked to yesterday—or someone in actual Faerie.'

The deep sinkhole drew Alfred's gaze. The distance to the

ground set off a flutter of butterflies in his belly. 'But to find the entrance, we have to get down there.'

'That's easy-peasy. We just need a long enough rope.' Saga pointed at the sinkhole rim.

In front of his feet, between the fence posts, steel rings had been hammered into the rock. They were meant for fastening climbing rope and had probably been used by search parties after disappearances, to rappel into the cave.

His eyes followed the perimeter of the sinkhole, and that's when he saw it. A familiar carved face, right next to where the creepers emerged. A forked tongue slid out of the mouth. The eyes opened. Alfred felt their stare. He couldn't breathe.

Behind him, Mr Tumbleweed shrieked, 'Aspy! Aspy! Herspy!' The twiggy limbs rattled.

Saga made soothing noises.

Alfred staggered back until he couldn't see the nightmare face any more. Until it couldn't see him.

What was that face doing here? Or, more importantly, what was it doing in Granny's cottage?

As Mr Tumbleweed calmed down, his shrieks became mutters. Alfred could make out the words. Over and over, the tree sprite murmured, 'A spy. Her spy.'

And whoever 'her' was, Alfred decided he had to get rid of the fork-tongued figurine in Granny's cottage. It had made him uncomfortable from the start. And it was someone's spy.

He took hold of the log that was the tree sprite's head and fixed his gaze on the black button-like eyes, asking, 'Who's spy?'

The buttons swished from side to side, before Mr Tumbleweed creaked, 'The queen's.'

'The queen's,' Alfred repeated.

'Is he talking about the faerie queen?' Saga asked.

But Mr Tumbleweed was shaking so much he couldn't answer.

From a nearby tree, Little Mother screeched, 'Oh, he'll be sorry now.'

Then a hailstorm of pinecones rained down on them.

'Sorry! This one body is sorry,' Mr Tumbleweed groaned, as they ran from the hard-hitting pellets.

The Monster Under the Bridge

They didn't stop running until they were some distance from the sinkhole.

'Okay,' Saga panted. 'Maybe not easy-peasy, if something's guarding the sinkhole.' She set Mr Tumbleweed down. 'But we'll find a way. There are coils of rope in the barn. If we tie them together, make some knots to help us climb down... and up. I can leave a note for Dad, so he knows where to find us if we can't get out again on our own.'

Alfred just nodded. He couldn't quite think about the logistics of getting into the sinkhole. His mind was full of horrible fork-tongued spies. Especially the one inside Granny's cottage.

He grabbed the twig arm of the tree sprite. 'Who is the queen? Where are her spies? Tell me!'

Mr Tumbleweed shook his log head. Fearfully, the button eyes flickered from tree to tree.

'Please, tell us,' Alfred said again.

The creature tried to shake Alfred off. When that didn't work, he covered his mouth with his other twig hand. Alfred prepared to remove the twigs, but the tree sprite did so himself, revealing what he'd done to his own face.

A layer of fresh bark had grown, closing the gash that had been his mouth. Rather than speak about the queen and her spy, he had literally sealed his lips.

'Is she really so frightening?'

Eyes flicking, Mr Tumbleweed gave a tiny nod.

Alfred let him go.

Saga held out her hand to her faerie companion. When he didn't take it, she said, 'We'll go the direct way home. It's much shorter from here. We just have to cross the river.'

As they walked, Alfred kept glancing back over his shoulder. Every little movement caught his gaze. Knots on the trees looked like eyes. Insects seemed to stretch into slithering tongues.

When he heard the babbles of the river, its music calmed him.

'There's the bridge,' Saga said. She strode towards the trunk of a fallen tree that lay across the river. Underneath, water rushed over boulders, cascading sprays into small waterfalls.

Mr Tumbleweed crossed in three big jumps.

The trunk was massive, but to Alfred it didn't seem like any kind of bridge. Moss and creepers covered it on all sides. They were soaked by the spray and probably slippery. The distance from bank to bank was at least three metres.

He couldn't remember ever walking as much as today. His ankles were sore and the muscles in his legs ached. Instead of trying to balance across, he wished he could swim.

Saga stepped up on the tree trunk and sauntered across, while Alfred stood on the brink and stared into the water. Downstream from the trunk, the water was deep. Turquoise threads flowed in rapid swirls. Below them, he could see something else. Long river weed strands. They snaked their way out of the river and up and down over the rocks.

'Are you coming?' Saga called from the other brink.

Alfred touched the little figurine in his pocket and his old medal for luck, placed the foot of his short leg on the trunk, and pushed off with the other. He wobbled, before he found his balance and began to shuffle across.

His eyes were drawn towards the water and the long weeds near the riverbed. He thought he saw the shadow of a large fish swimming under the trunk.

After a couple of steps, a single leaf fluttered down into the water. With a jerk, the strands came alive. They flowed upwards in bursts that caused small waves to form on the surface. Some snapped up above the water and whipped through the air.

He stopped. 'What's that?'

Saga didn't answer, but the way she was holding her kicking tree sprite told him it might be a faerie creature.

The water calmed again. He took another couple of careful steps.

A cramp was building in his short leg. As he put weight on it, his foot spasmed.

A clump of moss loosened. It rolled off the trunk, drifted down and floated on the water. One tendril of river weed broke the surface. It tentatively prodded the clump and the air surrounding it, like a hand searching in darkness.

Mr Tumbleweed's limbs were rattling so much Alfred could hear them.

A scatter of tiny pinpricks appeared on the water. Then long, slimy weeds exploded out of the river. In seconds, Alfred was tangled into strands which looped round his legs. He fell down onto his knees and hands. More weed tendrils wrapped themselves round his wrists. The strands pulled him towards the surface.

'Saga,' he croaked, but she was so distracted by the flailing tree sprite that she didn't hear.

He hugged the trunk, trying to push himself forward. Beneath him, the river began to bubble. Each bubble sprayed him with water when it burst.

'Saga!'

This time she heard him.

'Hold on!' She dropped Mr Tumbleweed. 'Lie still.'

'Some kind of monster is pulling me down.'

'I can see the water's bubbling. It might be a water sprite.'

A water sprite? Alfred thought about the woodcarving in his pocket. If this was a water sprite, then he wouldn't be scared. But what came out of the water bore no resemblance to the figurine.

First, enormous coils of slimy hair rose from the depths like an island rising out of receding tide. Then followed the head of a monster. Pointy ears stuck up among the tresses. The eyes emerged next. They were big, dark-green orbs that were staring right at him.

Alfred froze. He had never seen anyone look at him with such hatred.

The moment the mouth broke the surface, it opened in a bone-marrow-curdling screech. Slime dripped out between the many rows of sharp toothpick-like teeth. The screech went on and on until it almost sounded like a word. Until it sounded as if the creature screamed, 'YOUUUUU!'

His weed bindings tightened.

A webbed hand reached up out of the water, grabbed the slimy strands that were wrapped round Alfred, and with one tug pulled him off balance.

'Nemo!' Saga yelled.

It was the last thing he heard, before he plunged into the river and the water monster dragged him to the depths.

18

The Water Sprite in the River

Instinctively, Alfred closed his mouth, nose and eyes. He couldn't close his ears and he couldn't block the sound of the shriek with his fingers—his hands were tangled in the weeds that were the creature's hair.

When the monster stopped screeching, he heard the river's music all around him. The plinks of the sprays were like the delicate tones of an orchestra of tinkling bells. Swishing seagrass was the rattling percussion in the background. There was singing too. It made him want to dive deeper into the water. He almost forgot the monster.

Alfred tried to shake his head to stop himself from being swayed by the music. He wanted to listen to it for ever. He wanted to stay here, swimming in the river for ever.

The tension in his body evaporated. Letting himself relax, he floated with the tug of the hair strands. He had to get back to Saga, but a little longer under water would surely do him good.

Then a loud splash, like sudden crash cymbals, tore him out of the moment. Something landed right on top of him. He opened his eyes. Everything was as clear as if he'd worn swim goggles. By his side, Saga was holding on to his wrist, trying to haul him up to the surface. She clamped her nose with the fingers of her other hand, her cheeks bulging and full of air.

Hidden behind a blur of billowing curls, the creature swooped past Alfred. It grabbed Saga and pulled both of them along at high speed. They were coursing down the river, flowing fast downstream. He was being jostled by the hairs that bound him, and he kept being spiralled around. Saga looked like she was about to explode. He wished he could tell her to relax and still her heart, all the tricks he used himself when he was swimming under water.

His personal record was 6 minutes and 23 seconds, but Alfred knew he could hold his breath longer. When he set that record, he'd only surfaced because coach had sent two of his teammates down to the bottom of the pool to fetch him. How long would Saga last before she had to open her mouth?

Suddenly the creature inside the mass of curling hair propelled Saga up and out of the stream. Still bound, Alfred floated upwards with them. He got his head above the surface long enough to gulp air and see Saga sitting dazed on all fours with her mouth open, throwing up water.

When the monster dragged him back under, Alfred focused on slowing his pulse. He looked down at his arms. Long fingers gripped his shoulders from behind. The delicate hands weren't webbed. The strands of hair that snaked round his wrists didn't look slimy any more.

He tried to peek over his shoulder to see the monster, but too much hair got in the way. Some of it was his own, which appeared longer under water as the river straightened his curls. Most of it, though, was from the creature.

Down and down they went, in a river that seemed bottomless, until Alfred landed on solid ground. A puff of fine sand rose into a murky mist. A shoal of tiny fish surrounded him and nibbled at his fingers. They had greenish-brown backs and silvery sides with rows of black blotches. Behind them, the shadow of a much larger fish loomed.

'*Go, go. Go, go,*' the tiny fish sang, like a chorus.

Help me, Alfred thought.

As if they had understood, they began to nibble at the strands round his wrists.

'GO!' the monster bellowed, and the shoal dispersed.

The creature swam in front of him, but he still couldn't see it for all the hair. It was doing something to his legs. Perhaps anchoring him to a rock. Alfred tried to kick off from the ground. He wouldn't be able to hold his breath indefinitely. But it was no use. He began to panic. His pulse sped up.

Then he saw first one and then the other of his orthopaedic shoes drift away on the current, followed by his socks. The creature touched his toes. It stretched his legs out, until they were flat on the riverbed, one longer than the other.

'It *IS* you,' it sang. One of its hands brushed a mass of hair away, and with a speed that pushed water into his eyes so he had to close them, it flew straight for his face.

Alfred felt it hover inches away. He opened his eyes and got the biggest shock of the day. It was... She was—

He gasped.

Water streamed into his mouth, making him gulp. The river gurgled in his throat. He thrashed. Water kept pouring into his mouth. Somehow, he couldn't find the will to close it.

The river tasted like his favourite mint ice cream. No, better than that. Sweet and cooling and with a freshness that made him long for the next gulp. The sensation calmed him. The water caressed him outside and inside. It was wonderful.

Had he drowned?

As if watching himself from afar, he noticed how water flowed in through his mouth and out... It spurted out somewhere right in front of his ears, where he had those funny little indents, like misplaced dimples.

The water didn't enter his throat. It didn't fill his lungs. He could feel the current brush down the back of his neck.

Drifting, he became one with the river. The river was part of him, just like he was part of the river. He was home. This was where he belonged.

The creature floated upwards in front of him, keeping the same speed. She wasn't the monster he'd seen above the surface. Here, under water, underneath all the hair, she looked entirely different. Here, under water, she looked almost exactly like the water-sprite figurine in his pocket. She was beautiful.

He gazed into her green eyes. A range of emotions flitted across them. Surprise and wonder made him think he was seeing a reflection of his own feelings. But those expressions were quickly chased away by worry and a fear that he didn't feel any more.

'Just as reckless as Nereida,' the creature wailed. 'Just like her, trying to enter another realm.'

Her face contorted in furious anger and burning hatred. 'Don't ever come back,' she screeched.

They broke the surface together. She was the monster again, and with all her might she pushed Alfred so he flew up onto the bank.

A swirl of hair strands snapped like bullwhips over the water before she vanished.

And just like that, Alfred had been thrown out of the only space he'd ever felt he truly belonged.

19

A Hike Without Shoes

Alfred landed hard on his back. With a whoosh, the air in his lungs escaped his mouth. Above him, the treetops swirled on the blue sky.

'Nemo!' Saga's mouse-ear buns came into view. They dripped on him. 'I thought you'd drowned! What happened? Are you okay? You were down there for ages.'

He blinked. What *had* just happened?

'Let me help you.' Saga pulled his right leg up and placed his right hand against his left cheek. Before he could react, she'd rolled him into recovery position, saying, 'Just get it all out.'

But he didn't need to throw up. There was no river water in his stomach or anywhere else inside him. Still dazed, he rolled on until he was sitting sideways.

'I'm okay,' he croaked.

His hands flew to his ears. With two fingers, he felt around in front of them, fearing to find gaping holes. He found nothing except the two usual indents.

'Where are your shoes?'

Alfred looked down at his bare feet. The way he sat, sideways, his feet were perfectly aligned—not with the top foot sticking out like a person with equal length legs. It reminded him of the water-sprite figurine. He felt the outside of his pocket. It was still there. He hadn't lost it. Alfred wanted to take it out, see how much it resembled the creature in the river. At the same time, he never wanted to look at it again.

Quickly, he folded his knees up and hugged them. 'She took my shoes.'

'The water monster? Your socks too? Why would she do that?'

Why had she been so interested in his feet? 'You didn't see her, did you?'

Saga shook her head. 'There was too much sand and grit. I couldn't keep my eyes open. I probably wouldn't have seen her anyway.'

'She isn't a monster. Not under water. Well, perhaps she is. But she doesn't look like one. She looks like this.' He had to see how closely she resembled the figurine, and he brought it out. 'Like this water sprite.'

Saga leant over him, as Alfred studied the woodcarving. She had the same big round eyes, pointed ears and endlessly long hair as the real water sprite. But their other facial features differed, and the fierce anger he'd just seen could not be further from the figurine's sorrowful expression. When Saga reached out to touch her hair, Alfred stuffed the figurine back in his pocket.

'What happened down there?' Saga stared at him.

A faint echo of the underwater music still reached his ears. The dulcet tones called out to him. They wanted him to return. He wanted to return.

'I don't know,' he said. 'She was angry. After she took my shoes, she got angry. Didn't want me in the river. And she knew my mother. I think she knew my mother had entered

Faerie.' Alfred looked into the rushing water. There was no sight of weed-like hair now. The river wasn't deep—he could see the stones at the bottom. So how come he'd been far below the surface moments ago? Something about it was abnormal.

'Wait here.' Saga ran along the river to the tree trunk. Like him, she was drenched, but she'd had the sense to put her bag down before she jumped in the water. 'I'll look for rope when I get home,' she said upon her return. 'But it's too late to go back to the sinkhole today.'

When Saga whistled, Mr Tumbleweed sprang down from a tree and jumped ahead. Alfred followed the tree sprite, walking in front of Saga. He took care to place one foot on the warm dirt of the hollowed-out path and the other at the side in the moss, so it felt as if he was walking on a surface that fitted his legs. Even though he was mainly looking at the ground, he caught glimpses of knots on trees that looked like eyes and open mouths. Like spies.

After a while, they came in among pine trees, where both the path and the moss were littered with needles. The ones on the path lay flat, but the others prickled him. One of them got stuck in his foot, and he sat down on a boulder to extract it. It felt good to rest his legs. Above, a crow cawed.

'Don't lean back too far,' Saga said.

He half-turned on the boulder to see what she meant. Behind the low branches of a small tree, the ground vanished. He held on to the trunk of the tree and leant a bit further back. Below the vertical drop, he could just make out part of Granny's garden and a corner of the cottage roof. A crow swooped down towards him, cawing incessantly, until he pushed himself away from the edge.

When he turned round, Saga was standing over him.

She frowned. 'Your hair is longer.'

'It's just wet.' But it was almost dry by now, and Alfred knew it had grown. He'd felt it brush his shoulders. This morning the longest strands had just covered his ears. He swept it back, hoping that would make the change less conspicuous.

Saga narrowed her eyes and stared at the top of his tapered ears.

Before she could say anything, he got up and started down the steep path that ran along the cliff. He hated when people looked at him like he was an object to study.

On the rocky trail, his limp became more pronounced. Every step hurt from his feet up to his hips and lower back. He could feel Saga staring at him, at his limping legs, and he just wanted to get away from her.

Twice, she cleared her throat and said, 'Nemo,' but he ignored her and kept walking.

The ground was flattening out when he stumbled over a tree root. He fell hard on his hands. One knee landed on stone.

'Are you okay?' Saga held out a hand to help him up.

He ignored it and stayed sitting, massaging his sore leg muscles.

'Is something wrong with your legs?'

'I can hardly walk without my shoes, and you hadn't noticed?' he snapped.

Saga shrugged.

At least she had asked. Most people just looked away if he caught them staring. 'My right leg's 5.3 centimetres shorter than the left.'

'Oh, that must be so annoying. What do the doctors say? Can't they operate? Or do they have to wait until you're a grown-up?'

'I've never been to see a doctor.'

'Not ever? Not even for vaccinations?'

'Not that I remember.' Was that odd? Did people see doctors if they weren't ill?

She crouched in front of him, peering at him as if he were a puzzle to solve, then nodding as if a piece had fallen into place.

'Why are you looking at me like that?

'It's just... I think... Perhaps... Have you considered that you might be a faerie?'

'What?'

'You can see them and talk to them. They seem to know who you are. Amanita did. And the water sprite recognized you too.'

'You've met my dad. Does he look like a faerie?'

'No, I mean...' Saga pushed her glasses up. Her enlarged eyes blinked once. 'You could be a changeling.'

20

A Faerie Changeling

'A changeling?' Alfred stood up and crossed his arms.

Behind Saga, Mr Tumbleweed shook his head.

'You know, switched,' Saga said, stretching out of the crouch. 'Sometimes faeries will exchange one of their own children for a human baby. In stories, the faerie child usually ages really fast or is sickly and dies... You could be an exception...'

'But then my dad wouldn't be my dad, would he?'

'Oh, I hadn't thought about that. But you could have the most interesting faerie parents—'

'And why would those interesting faerie parents want a human child to replace their own?'

'There could be any number of reasons, perhaps their own child was ugly or looked different—'

'With a limb length discrepancy? That's the official term, in case you were wondering.' Alfred turned and stalked away, his limp worse than ever. He didn't want to hear any more of Saga's ridiculous theories.

'That's not what I meant. Perhaps you looked too human for them. I can understand your leg thing is frustrating for you, but why would anyone else care?' She followed close on his heels. 'They might have needed a human child for some kind of faerie magic and had to hand over their own beloved baby in exchange.' She talked faster and faster. 'I'm not saying your faerie parents wanted to give you away. Maybe they were forced to do so by that evil faerie queen! Maybe she tricked them into promising their firstborn... They could have tried to escape and fought against giving you up. Perhaps they...' She kept finding hypothetical explanations, but Alfred wasn't listening any more.

It all made a strange kind of sense.

It wasn't just his leg that was different. He'd always felt different. Some people said he had his dad's mouth and chin, but that was where the similarities stopped. Personality-wise they were nothing alike. And Alfred's eyes weren't blue like Dad's. They were green, like the water sprite's eyes. Like Nereida's, according to Granny.

He slowed and looked back over his shoulder. 'Or,' he said, interrupting Saga's monologue. 'Maybe Nereida's a faerie.'

'That's impossible!' In the patient tone of someone explaining to a small child, she continued, 'Your granny and your dad might have the sight, but my mum and everyone else wouldn't have been able to see Nereida if she's a faerie, would they?'

'But why can they see me, if I'm a faerie?'

'I said "changeling". In all the stories I've read, people can see changelings. They're enchanted to look human, so their human parents take care of them.' Saga overtook him, and he limped after her.

Thankfully, she stopped talking. He needed to concentrate on the vortex of thoughts that whirled inside his mind.

If he was a changeling, then the faeries had stolen Nereida and Dad's baby. Had Nereida gone into the faerie realm to find her real human son? Was that why the water sprite called her reckless?

The water sprite had known who he was after studying his legs. What if that terrifying creature was his biological mother? It would certainly explain his swimming abilities.

But if Dad wasn't his father and Granny wasn't his grandmother, then he had no clue who he was himself. In trying to find his mother, had he made everything worse?

They were heading out of the forest, but Alfred felt he'd never been so deep in the woods.

'Wait,' Saga said when they reached the last trees. 'D'you want me to cut your hair? So your grandmother doesn't notice...' She trailed off.

He stopped. 'You don't think the fact that I'm drenched and shoeless is enough to distract her?'

'Fine. Just make sure you collect all the hair you snip off when you cut it. Leave nothing for the faeries to get hold of.'

They stood side by side above the meadow of wildflowers, where Alfred had first seen traces of Little Mother and Little Father.

'Do you think I wear my hair like this to make a fashion statement?' Saga pointed at the two buns on top of her head and the two buns by her neck. 'This way, if a hair falls out, I won't just lose it in the forest for them to pick up. Faeries can get power over you if they own part of you—even something as small as a nail clipping. That's what the books say.' She fished a couple of scrunchies out of her shoulder bag. 'Perhaps it's actually safer if you keep it long and use some of these.'

'Does it matter, if I'm a faerie too?' Alfred asked, but he pocketed a green hairband. He imagined the little people scouring Granny's garden for anything they could use against him.

'Even if you're a faerie, I hope we're still friends.'

Friends. He supposed they were friends. There was something about the way Saga accepted him as he was that made him want to be her friend. He felt a twinge of guilt. She was an open book, telling him everything that went through her mind. Inside him, thoughts churned. Only few of them made it out into the open. He hadn't told her about breathing under water, and he hadn't even trusted her enough to let her hold the water-sprite figurine.

He nodded.

'I hope you are a faerie, because that should make it much easier for you to persuade the other faeries to help us stop the tunnel project.' She set off downhill towards the farm.

Alfred took his phone out of his back pocket. It didn't appear to be damaged after having been in the river, and it had network. Two small bars, but that was enough for a voice call.

Saga turned back. 'Are you okay?'

'Yeah, yes. I just need a moment.'

'D'you want me to stay?'

He shook his head.

'Okay, see you tomorrow.' In puffs of dandelion clocks, she ran downhill through the meadow, chased by Mr Tumbleweed.

Alfred sank down in the long grass. He dialled three times before Dad picked up.

'What happened? Are you okay? Is it Granny?' Dad sounded breathless. There were voices in the background. 'Let me just close the door.'

'I need to ask you something.'

'Now, Alfie? Does it have to be right now? I'm in a meeting.'

'Yes. Or it can wait until tonight if you could come to the cottage...'

'I can't. I'll be working all weekend. We're going over the geological findings. There are some puzzling things. Data that should've been double-checked. We can't start drilling if we risk the whole hill collapsing on our heads.'

'So you can't start drilling on Monday?'

'We have to start on Monday. That mole costs thousands a day. And because of all the accidents and delays, the budget is already squeezed. I have to sort this out. Unless I find a reason, we can't delay any longer.'

'Does the data have anything to do with the sinkholes?' Alfred asked, wondering if Dad was actively looking for a reason to delay. Perhaps they were on the same side.

'The sinkholes?'

'I know about... my mother. I know she disappeared.'

The silence at the other end of the line was so long, Alfred thought he'd lost the connection. Then Dad said, 'You know...' into another silence.

'I found the gravestone. I persuaded Granny to tell me,' Alfred said, feeling strangely defensive about knowing. 'I want to hear about it from you. It doesn't have to be right now. Will you promise to tell me?'

'Yes.'

'You have to save the Faerie Hill! What if she's still somewhere inside?'

'Oh, Alfie, she can't be.' Dad's voice was oddly choked. Alfred could easily imagine the painful expression in his eyes, because he'd seen it every time he asked about his mother. 'I really have to go.'

'Wait.' Alfred hesitated. If he didn't ask now, he would lose courage. But suddenly he couldn't find the words. He couldn't just say, 'Are you sure I'm your real son?' Instead, he blurted out, 'Why did you never get my leg operated?'

'Alfie...'

'I just want to know why.'

Dad sighed. 'I promised myself I wouldn't let anyone operate on you.'

'Why? That doesn't make sense.'

'Alright. I promised Nereida. I promised her never to take you to a doctor unless your life was threatened.'

His father's use of his mother's name left him speechless. *When* had Dad made that promise? Was it before Alfred was born or after she'd discovered he was a changeling? Granny had said Nereida was worried about something before she disappeared. Had she thought a doctor would find out he wasn't human? Why had she cared, if he wasn't even her son, but the son of a faerie who'd abducted her child?

'I'm sorry, Alfie. I really have to go.'

'Did she know about my leg?'

'Of course she knew. It's a congenital—'

'But did you notice right after I was born?' That would be the absolute proof he wasn't a changeling.

As if his father had realized he wouldn't be able to duck the question, he sighed and started talking. 'You have to understand... It was a difficult birth. Even Vera, who is an advocate for home births, wanted to deliver you in the hospital, but Nereida wouldn't hear of it. She wouldn't leave the cottage. You seemed fine—passed all the preliminary tests—so Vera concentrated on your mother... Perhaps it was too much for Vera, because she went into labour herself the next day and then—what's her name? Something with L...'

'Saga. That's what she calls herself now.' For a brief moment, he wondered about Saga's real name. Laura, Lena, Liz?

'When Vera saw you, a couple of days later, she couldn't understand how she could've missed it...'

'When did you notice?'

'I don't remember, Alfie. So much happened around that time...'

'But before my... Nereida disappeared?'

'Oh, yes. You were not more than a day or two old when she pointed it out to me.'

'Did she mind?' he asked, but his thoughts were racing ahead. The faeries could've switched him during those first days. There was no proof he wasn't a changeling.

'Oh, Alfie, what's brought this on? Of course she didn't mind. She loved you from the moment she first saw you. As did I. You know that, right? I love you, and I'm sorry I can't be there right now. As soon as I figure out what's going on with this geo dataset... I'll try to come tomorrow or at the latest Sunday, is that okay?'

Alfred nodded, then remembered Dad couldn't see him. 'Okay, Dad.'

'I love you, okay? Get Granny to give you a hug from me,' he said and hung up.

And it was kind of okay. Talking to Dad had loosened a tension deep inside Alfred's gut.

Perhaps Saga was right, perhaps he really was a faerie changeling. But even if he had been switched as a baby, Dad was still his dad.

 21

The Underground Stream

Everything hurt as Alfred walked the last stretch to the cottage.

It was only when he entered the garden that he decided he wouldn't cut his hair. He wanted to see Granny's reaction to its length. Perhaps a little shock would make her remember more than Dad about those first days of his life.

The door to the shed was open. She would be in there with her yarns. That gave him an opportunity to change clothes and find some shoes before she saw him. Alfred wanted nothing to distract her from his hair.

He was so preoccupied by this plan, that he'd almost reached the front steps before he remembered the fork-tongued figurine above the door. It looked exactly like the face at the rim of the sinkhole. And Mr Tumbleweed had reacted just as he did at the sinkhole when he saw this figurine. The nightmarish woodcarving had to be a spy. A spy for the faerie queen.

Was it spying on Granny? Reporting somehow, perhaps with the help of the crows, on everything that went on in the cottage? The crows certainly reacted to him, he thought, glancing up at the cawing flock of black birds.

Unnoticed, at least by Granny, he slipped inside. He made for her bedroom where he placed the water-sprite figurine behind the lamp on her bedside table and forced his fingers to let go.

In his own room, he changed into a dry T-shirt and jeans. The bruise on his knee was already turning blue. Even after he rinsed his feet, the soles remained dirty, with reddish swellings and a blister under his left big toe. It was a strange sight—he'd never walked barefoot outdoors before. It hurt when he put on shoes. His left knee and hip hurt even more when he stood up, and all the muscles in both legs were sore.

Outside again, Alfred pretended to be coming home.

'Granny!' he called as he approached the shed.

'In here,' she answered.

Alfred ducked into the bright light of the cave. She was standing by the gas stove, stirring something in the huge pot.

'Did you have a nice day?' she asked.

'Yeah.'

'Can you bring me the bowl with the onion skins? I have artichokes in here, but I want this green to be more yellow.'

Without looking up, she took a handful of the crisp brown skins and crushed them over the pot. 'The protest was a disaster, of course. And that horrible mayor. Did you get a chance to see your father?'

'Nah. I just went with Saga.' Before Granny could ask where he and Saga had gone, he added, 'The little people are angry about the tunnel.'

'I know.' She sighed and covered the pot with a lid. 'Let's have a cup of tea and talk about it. I've baked blueberry muffins.'

Alfred's stomach growled in response. He hadn't eaten anything since breakfast. 'That sounds great.' Granny still hadn't looked at him. But there was no rush. She'd see his hair when they sat across from each other in the kitchen.

'I just need to check on the foxglove bath—they give the most wonderful apple green colour,' Granny muttered. 'The colour of hope. We could all use that right now.'

He passed all the troughs and crouched by the stream. The industrial light cast his shadow into the darkness. The spring trickled, in a faint echo of the river's music.

'Nereida,' Granny said behind him, her voice a hoarse whisper.

Alfred spun towards her, his long hair swishing.

'Oh, my heart... I could swear...' Granny was clutching a bundle to her chest. Her breaths came in sharp puffs. 'Your hair!' The wet yarn was dripping on Granny's legs and the floor. The front of her coverall was already soaked. 'I think I need to sit down.'

Alfred was by her side in a couple of steps, regretting now that he'd wanted to shock her. She was staring at him as if for the first time. He took the bundle from her, asking, 'Does this go in here?'

When she nodded, he dropped it in the dye bath. Granny clutched his arm, as he led her to a chair by her worktable.

'She used to sit just like that when she was pregnant. Right there, looking into the water. For hours. Just for a moment, I thought...' Granny took a deep breath.

'Here.' Alfred held a mug with leftover tea towards her.

Granny sipped the tea and grimaced

'I look like Nereida? My mother, Nereida?'

'Do you know any other Nereida?'

Alfred shook his head. 'Are you okay, Granny?'

'I'm fine now.' She took another sip and looked at her watch. 'Goodness it's late. Come. We might be on the local news at seven thirty. Let's make an omelette. Then we can have the muffins for dessert.'

Alfred walked next to Granny into the cottage, a hand by her elbow in case she should need support. He then stayed in the kitchen to keep an eye on her, and helped chop mushrooms and ham for the omelette. But she seemed to have recovered.

In the front room, they moved the tangle of yarn to the armchair so they could have dinner at the sofa table and watch the news on what Alfred was sure must be the world's smallest telly.

While he stuffed himself, he kept glancing at Granny. Did they have the same chin? Her nose was wider and shorter than his, her eyes a clear blue. There was an old photo of his grandfather in the bookcase. He'd died before Alfred was born, but he resembled Dad.

Alfred wished he could ask Granny if she'd ever suspected he was a changeling and tell her about the water sprite in the river. But telling her might give her an even bigger shock. And if she knew what he and Saga were planning, she would without doubt forbid him from going into the woods.

The brief reportage from the protest focused on Saga and her run to the cliff. In one shot, Alfred could just make out his own face, with his much shorter hair, behind her.

'Do I really look like Nereida?' he asked when the weather forecast began.

'Of course you do,' Granny said, stacking the dishes onto a tray.

'Don't you have a photo of her? Dad has thrown all his away.'

A worried look came into her eyes. 'He hasn't. Although your father is so good at throwing things away. It's a great skill to have when you move around so much.'

'He hasn't?'

Granny continued talking as if she hadn't heard him. 'Do you remember when he'd thrown your teddy away, because you decided you were too big for soft toys? It only lasted a week. We were so lucky they still had the same one in the toyshop in town.'

She was changing the subject away from Nereida again.

'What do you mean, he hasn't thrown the photos away?'

She sighed. 'There weren't any. She never wanted to have her photo taken.'

'Why? Was she afraid the faeries would steal them?' he asked, wondering if it was risky, like if they got hold of your hair or nail clippings.

'There are so many superstitions, it's hard to know which ones to believe.' Granny got up with the tray. 'Goodness, I've forgotten the milk,' she called from the hallway. 'And the shed door. Where's my head tonight?'

'I'll do it, Granny.'

Trying to hide his worsened limp, Alfred walked past the kitchen window, balancing the dish full of milk. He pushed it under the rose hedge, saying, 'Here you go.'

No little people answered from under the brambles.

Inside the cave, without Granny bustling about, the water's music was much clearer. Alfred limped back to the pole with its hooks and hanks of hanging yarn.

He crouched by the spring, where he'd sat when Granny mistook him for Nereida. How could he be a changeling if he looked so much like her? Unless the faeries had somehow enchanted him to look like her... Perhaps he'd lived his whole life disguised by a layer of glamour.

The spring tinkled. He wished he could stick his head underwater to hear the music properly, but the little stream wasn't more than a handbreadth deep.

His fingers hovered above the surface, before he plunged them into the cool flow. The spring's music vibrated up his wrists.

Suddenly, he heard a rushing from the darkness. The water rose, as if called by his touch. The depth of the stream quadrupled. Into view sailed first one, then the other, of his shoes. He rescued them, while the water sank again. His socks didn't appear.

The arrival of his shoes told him three things. Firstly, that a connection existed between the river and Granny's spring. Secondly, that the tunnel was at least big enough for his shoes to get through. Thirdly, and worst of all, that the monstrous water sprite knew exactly where he lived.

With his wet shoes in one hand, he turned off the lights. As if it were fluorescent, the spring cast a blueish tinge over everything. It continued far beyond the part of the cave Granny used... All the way to the creature that had looked at Alfred with such anger and hatred.

Outside, he slid the two heavy metal bolts into place. It was no wonder Granny kept the entry to the cave locked.

22

The Best Gift

Alfred was so exhausted he didn't get up until just before noon the next day. The cottage was silent.

In the early morning, Granny had been in his room. He'd mumbled that he wanted to sleep and and said no when she offered to stay home from the market. More asleep than awake, he'd heard her potter around. Before she left, she'd been muttering about his wet shoes and bringing a box of his dad's old comics down from the loft.

His legs were stiff and sore as he got up and staggered to the bathroom. On the warm radiator, his high-top trainers, stuffed with paper towels, were almost dry.

After washing his hands, he stared at himself in the mirror. At his hair. It had never been this long. When he brushed it back into a short ponytail, the tips of his ears poked out. Tapered faerie ears. Swimming caps had been hiding them for years. While he pulled at the funny dimples in front of them, he turned his head from side to side. Staring into his own green eyes, he saw the water sprite's orbs reflected back.

Did faeries choose changeling foster parents based on looks? Or had they really enchanted him to resemble Nereida?

Alfred narrowed his eyes and unfocused his gaze, in an effort to look past any layer of glamour. Unsurprisingly, his appearance in the mirror didn't change.

Nereida must've known, though. Had she taken one look at him and seen he was a changeling? She couldn't have told Dad or Granny—the people he called Dad and Granny—or they wouldn't have brought him up as their own.

The phone in the kitchen rang, and he lurched away from his own reflection.

'Your granny called to say you were knackered and not to ring you before noon. It's three minutes past, now,' Saga said without preamble. 'There's an emergency meeting about the tunnel at two. Are you coming?'

'No... I—'

'It's okay. But by the time the meeting finishes, it'll be too late to go to the sinkhole. Do you mind if we wait until tomorrow?'

'Not at all. My legs are so sore.'

'Mine too. I'll pick you up at nine.'

Before he could answer, Saga had hung up again.

Alfred let his breath out in a deep sigh. One more day of respite. It wasn't even the walking that bothered him most. He was suddenly scared of going to Faerie. What if he found his faerie parents and they wanted nothing to do with him? Or, even worse, what if his new-found parents begged him to stay? He couldn't just leave Dad.

After pouring himself a glass of milk, Alfred sank down on a chair. Next to the basket with bread and leftover muffins lay a small, gift-wrapped box and a folded note.

The note was written in Granny's sprawling cursive. He deciphered it to say, *Your mother would have wanted you to have this when you were old enough. I'll be back by five. Love, Granny.*

Inside the box, silk paper unfurled to reveal the water-sprite figurine.

Alfred smiled. He felt like whooping. Her sorrowful expression remained unchanged. The resin tear glistened. When he held her and stroked her hair, the familiar feeling of warmth spread inside him.

While he buttered a slice of bread and slathered it with Granny's rose hip jam, he set her down and studied the fine details of the woodcarving.

To think it was a gift from his mother, he thought, before he remembered that Nereida wasn't his mother. Perhaps this was her way of giving him a clue about his faerie parents.

Clutching the figurine in one hand, he ate his bread, drank his milk and picked at a muffin. No matter what or who she represented, she was the best gift he'd ever received.

The rest of the afternoon, he lay on his bed, reading Dad's old comic books, trying hard not to think. Holding the water sprite kept his dread at bay, and he wished he could just forget about everything and stay like this all week, doing nothing.

At five, Granny came home from the market with sausages for dinner and a blinding headache.

'I didn't sleep much last night,' she said with a sideways glance at his long hair.

When Alfred thanked her for the figurine she smiled weakly, while kneading her temples. 'I'm sorry to see her go, but she belongs with you, dear.' She pushed her plate of uneaten food away. 'I think I need to lie down in a dark room.'

Alfred offered to do the dishes and put out the milk, and she went straight to bed. So did he, after he'd finished the chores.

Gazing up at the tapestry in the semi-darkness, Alfred clasped the water sprite again. She was his for ever and ever, and he never wanted to let go.

She made him feel better, perhaps like an actual mother would. She also gave him courage. Courage to go with Saga tomorrow, even though he was afraid of what he would find in Faerie.

23

An Invasion of Ivy

The next morning, Granny was back to her usual bustling self. Between her leaving for the market and Saga arriving to pick him up, Alfred had ten minutes to get ready.

After brushing his teeth, he ran outside to search the stacked firewood next to the shed. The logs were too big, but he found a suitable piece of kindling and hacked the stick in half with Granny's small axe. It would have to do.

Inside again, he climbed up on the stool in the hallway. The spy figurine above the door was right at eye-level, its forked tongue lolling out.

Hastily, he drew a red wool sock, which he'd borrowed from the laundry line, down over the scary face. A vibration ran up his arm. He stuffed the sock-covered figurine in his spare trouser pocket and took a moment to position the stick in its stead. At a quick glance, Granny wouldn't notice it was missing. And once she did, he would come up with an explanation. As soon as he got to the forest, he would bury it or hide it so it couldn't ever spy on him or Granny again.

While he locked the door, Alfred noticed the quietness. Not a leaf moved in the still air. The woodcarvings in the front windows seemed lifeless. His neck didn't prickle as he walked down the garden path.

By the gate, he glanced back. From this distance, the stick had the size and shape of the fork-tongue carving. Still, something about the cottage and the garden was odd. Something was missing. His eyes did a sweeping check. The windows were closed, and the shed door was bolted. Atop the limestone wall, the trees swayed. Perhaps it was simply that he didn't feel the intimidating glare of the spy?

Saga and Alfred cycled together to the track up to the tunnel building site. From that side of the hill, they wouldn't have to cross the river in the middle of the woods, and the path was less steep. A coiled rope filled most of Saga's basket. On top, Mr Tumbleweed held himself and her shoulder bag in place.

Saga was telling Alfred about the disastrous nature group meeting where all the adults had given up the fight.

'It's a good thing you can talk to faeries,' she said, 'because they're our last hope. And today might be our last chance to get into the faerie realm! Have you thought about that?' She looked sideways at him. Her bicycle swerved. Mr Tumbleweed clutched at the basket and gave an angry snort. 'That horrible drill or mole or whatever you call it might cause the underground to collapse. It might destroy the entrance to Faerie.'

Alfred just nodded. Everything Saga said increased his sense that something was wrong.

They left their bikes and crawled through the gap in the scrub to the pond. That was where Alfred realized what had been missing in Granny's garden. The air above the pond was alive with buzzing insects and birds, whereas at the cottage...

Nowhere—not in the garden, not perched on the thatched roof, not cawing from the trees—had he seen a single crow. Although he wasn't fond of the black birds, it made him uneasy. He imagined voices hissing, 'He'll be sorry'.

Trying to shake the sense of foreboding, he asked Saga about the otters. He trudged uphill after her, while she raved about seeing otter pups the previous year. Above her red and purple striped leggings and inside-out top, her four ginger buns bounced with every step. She'd already checked his hairband was securely fastened.

At the top of the hillock, she stopped so abruptly he walked into her. He repositioned the rope he was carrying. And then they just stood and gaped at the office containers, the bulldozers, the excavators and the rest of the machinery. Or rather, at their shapes.

It was as if someone had thrown a green blanket over a floor scattered with toys. The ivy-like vines they had seen emerge from the sinkhole had crept out of the forest and down the steep cliff face.

'Do you think the faeries heard us the other day?' Saga asked. 'Is this their way of helping?'

Mr Tumbleweed's eyes shone with mirth.

'Maybe.'

Below them, the signs and barricades had sunk beneath the sea of plants. The construction vehicles were huge green mounds, with only a few visible gleams of yellow paint. And the living greenery entangled the office containers.

'I don't think it's enough,' Saga said. 'This won't delay the project for more than a few days. But the fact that the faeries are doing something... That must mean they are willing to help.'

They followed the trail, which luckily didn't lead directly up to the woods, or it would've been buried under the creepers. Alfred's knees and muscles already ached.

The forest seemed different. Looming and hushed, without any birdsong, the trees rose around them. The only sounds were the creaks when Mr Tumbleweed hopped and the rustle of the vines as they slid over dead leaves.

At the sinkhole, layers of the climbing creepers grew out of the deep cavity. They emerged in jerks and covered half the perimeter.

Alfred let the rope fall by the steel rings on the other side of the rim. From across the sinkhole, the upward motion of the plants reminded him of a slow-motion video clip of a waterfall in reverse he'd once seen. To his relief, this green river hid the face of the spy.

Leaning on the part of the fence that was still intact, they stood looking down into the cavern. It did not look inviting. Even if he and Saga made it down, they had to get past the poisonous vines without touching them. Saga's fingertips were still red and blistered after their contact with a single leaf.

'Before we go down there, perhaps we should ask that Amanita if the faeries want to collaborate,' Saga said, rubbing her fingertips.

'D'you think she'll come if I call her name?'

'Only one way to find out. But you have to be really, really careful. I can't hear her, so you'll have to tell me everything she says and let me help you with answers.'

'I'll be like an interpreter!' Alfred pushed himself up on the top bar of the fence, so his arms bore his weight and his feet dangled above the ground. It felt good to relieve his legs.

'No, you won't, because she'll be trying to trick you.'

'She seemed nice.'

'But if she thinks we're asking for a favour... We don't want to be indebted to a faerie. She'll ask for something in return. They always do that in books. Something you think is minor, but before you know it, you've pledged your firstborn—'

Suddenly, what felt like a tree branch landed on Alfred's back. His back that was leaning out over the fence. It pushed him off balance. The top bar squeezed his stomach. He swung down until his face was below his feet. Upside-down, he saw them kicking in the air.

The thing on his back snorted.

Someone somewhere screeched, 'Who's sorry now?'

'Get off him!' Saga yelled. 'Get off him, Mr Tumbleweed!' As she got hold of the tree sprite, the weight that had forced him down lifted from Alfred's back. With Saga's help, he pulled himself back to safety.

She turned to Mr Tumbleweed, who lay in a heap of sticks on the ground where she'd thrown him, yelling, 'What are you doing?'

'Wait, Saga—' Alfred wanted to say that perhaps the little people had been behind this too, but she wasn't listening.

Raging, Saga advanced on the tree sprite. 'First the branch, now this. Are you trying to kill my friend? Go away! Get away from us! Go away!'

Mr Tumbleweed freed himself from the loose sticks and backed away. His black button eyes gleamed. With one of his twig fingers, he sliced the new bark, opening the gash that was his mouth.

When he spoke, his groaning voice was loud and clear. But before Alfred could react to the words, Mr Tumbleweed leapt up on the fence and jumped into the sinkhole.

24

A Faerie Deal

Saga ran to the fence, reaching, grabbing at the empty air next to Alfred.

They watched in horror as the little creature slammed onto the ground thirty metres beneath them.

Saga inhaled sharply.

Below, Mr Tumbleweed bounced, as if he'd landed on a trampoline. He grinned up at them and waved, before he sprang out of sight, behind the curtain of vines.

They remained standing, looking into the sinkhole, until Saga asked, 'What did he say? Is he looking for the entrance to Faerie? Should we get the rope ready?'

It was moments before Alfred answered, because he'd heard exactly what Mr Tumbleweed had said, and he didn't quite know how to tell Saga. Whether the little people had thrown the tree sprite onto Alfred's back or not didn't matter.

He cleared his throat. 'Er... He said "Thank you, silly child, for freeing me from the bond."'

'I banished him?' Saga sank down until she was crouched, leaning her forehead against the fence post. 'I think I banished him.' Her voice was muffled. 'He... He might never come back.'

'You don't know that.' Alfred gave her a little pat on the shoulder. After a while, he added, 'Perhaps the fact he jumped into the sinkhole is proof that's where the entrance is. But I still think we should try to call Amanita first.'

When she didn't answer, Alfred turned and called the faerie.

He only called once, and then, as if she'd been observing them, Amanita stepped out from behind a nearby tree. Her moss-green skirt swished. Dewdrops on its hem glittered. Like buttons, a line of white-speckled red toadstools ran from her neckline to the ground.

'Hello again... Nemo,' she said. 'And your little friend is here too. How delightful!'

Saga scrambled to her feet. She took hold of Alfred's wrist and leant towards him. 'I can see her. And hear her,' she whispered so quietly her words were a mere breath on his cheek.

'Interesting. Something must've changed.' Amanita's eyes swept over them. 'I wonder...'

Mr Tumbleweed is gone, Alfred thought. Perhaps he'd been preventing Saga from seeing other faeries all these years.

Saga let go of Alfred, straightened, and said in a clear voice, 'I'm Saga.'

'Of course you are,' Amanita said. 'The invisible girl. You are a legend in these parts of the woods. You and your tree sprite. Where is that little grump?'

When Saga said nothing, Alfred began, 'He's—' but Saga interrupted him.

'—somewhere nearby. We wanted to ask you about working together. We saw the vines...'

Amanita cocked her head. Her long birch-bark hair hung loose today, only held by a pair of matching light-blue butterfly hair clips. At her movement, a few strands of hair escaped. She lifted a hand, as if to push them away from her face, but before her hand passed her shoulder, one of the butterflies had already fluttered down past her brow.

It extended slender arms round the hairs and flew with them back up on top of Amanita's head. It wasn't a butterfly at all, but a tiny, winged faerie. Hair-thin antenna came out of its forehead. They vibrated. With fear, Alfred thought. What was it doing here as a hairpiece on another faerie?

'The vines?' Amanita smiled.

'Those ones.' Saga pointed behind them at the river of creepers. 'They've been sent by you, haven't they? By the faeries, I mean? They are growing out of Faerie, right?'

'We've just come from the tunnel building site,' Alfred said. 'All the equipment is covered by those plants. They aren't supposed to be there.'

'Oh, I agree,' Amanita replied. 'The weight of that heavy machinery on the realm alone is enough to anger us. We are... The queen is exceptionally annoyed.'

'So the plants are there on purpose to stop the tunnel project?'

'But it's not enough,' Saga said. 'It'll only delay the workers until they've killed your plants. We need to do more.'

'Never fear for our plants. They will kill humans before they are killed.' A sharp edge had come into Amanita's voice. 'And we will do more.'

The plants were not only poisonous, they were deadly. Alfred suddenly felt cold. 'More, like what?'

'Floods. Fires. Infestations. Anything that only affects the surface.'

'But that will harm nature too,' Saga said, at the same time as Alfred asked, 'Infestations?'

Amanita flicked her fingers at one of her red buttons. It landed on the ground. Within seconds, hundreds of toadstools popped up, covering the moss.

'And my father...' Dad would be at the building site tomorrow morning, before the mole arrived. He would want to clear away the plants. Would he consider that they might be poisonous before touching them?

'I thought it was your mother you wanted to find,' Amanita said in a sweet tone, as if she hadn't just threatened them with killer plants and other faerie enchantments that caused death and destruction.

'I did. I do. But we have to stop the tunnel without harming people.'

'And nature,' Saga added.

'Come with me to our realm, Nemo. You can help us find a way.'

Alfred nodded. Humans and faeries should find a solution together.

'I'm afraid you can't bring your friend.' Amanita held a pale hand out to him. Like a bracelet in perpetual motion, a small snake with a zigzag pattern on its back chased its own tail round her wrist.

'Then he isn't going,' Saga said.

'Then I'm not going,' Alfred repeated, although he wanted to go with the faerie.

'What a pity.' Amanita stepped closer to Alfred and laid a hand on his shoulder. A shiver went through him as the snake brushed against his T-shirt. Gently, she said, 'I thought finding your mother mattered to you.'

'It does.'

'Then take a little walk with me. I promise we will stay in this world.' Amanita swept her hand in a graceful motion, indicating a path between the nearest trees. 'Alone.'

'It's okay for Saga to hear what you have to say.'

'I'm afraid it is not. So we shall have to speak another time... Nemo.'

She started to turn away, but Alfred called. 'No, wait!' And to Saga, 'Stay here.'

'Very well.' With a deep sigh and another swirling hand gesture, Amanita strode in among the trees.

Alfred ran to catch up with her. They had to find another solution to the tunnel problem, otherwise Dad and many others would be in danger. But he also wanted information about his faerie parents.

'Be careful!' Saga called from behind.

'Are my parents still there in your realm?' he blurted out when he'd overtaken Amanita.

'My, my, you are eager. It must be your faerie blood.'

'The water sprite in the river isn't my mother, is she?' It wasn't the question he had planned to ask, but the words 'your faerie blood' echoed in his mind. The echo increased until the voice in his head shouted *'Faerie blood!'*

He had to concentrate. Saga would be cross with him if he didn't think carefully about what he was asking. But if he found out that creature was his mother... that would be even worse than never discovering who his mother was. 'It can't be her. She tried to drown me.'

Amanita stopped walking. 'Did she really?' There was a strange gleam in her eyes. 'That is interesting.'

'But she isn't my mother, is she?' he repeated.

'No. And you should stay away from her. She is dangerous, as are many other creatures here and in the realm. You need protection. We would not want you to get hurt.'

'What about all the people that'll get hurt by those poisonous vines?'

Amanita shrugged, as if their lives didn't matter. The butterfly faeries in her hair fluttered. 'Come with me. Should we find another way to stop the destruction, our plants will be called home.'

'But will you tell me who my parents are first?'

'There are rules. I'm afraid I cannot answer any more questions without payment.'

'What kind of payment?' A knot tightened in Alfred's belly. Was he about to be tricked like Saga had foreseen? He desperately wished she was by his side.

'You have something the queen wants,' Amanita said. 'In your pocket, if I'm not mistaken.'

How did Amanita know what was in his pocket? He'd thought one figurine would be protected by the red sock and the other by the iron in his old medal. It could only be because the real water sprite had seen the figurine when he fell in the river. 'Is she... Is the water sprite... Is she the queen?'

'Lillith?' Amanita let out a burst of laughter. It sounded like a tinkle of bells that called you nearer. 'A mere water sprite as queen? I have never heard anything so absurd.' She laughed again and shook her head. One of the butterfly-faeries snatched at an escaping strand of hair.

Lillith, Alfred thought. He knew her name now, and names had power according to Saga.

'The queen is the most powerful and beautiful faerie you will ever see.'

Amanita had seemed so nice at first, but there was something menacing about her now, and the way she spoke about the queen... It sounded as if she worshipped the faerie queen.

Lillith must have reported seeing the water-sprite figurine. That was the only possible explanation for the queen knowing he had it. But he wouldn't ever give it away. However, he also carried the fork-tongued spy in a pocket. If the queen had spies everywhere already, giving her one more couldn't hurt. And he wouldn't be sad to let that figurine go.

Alfred stuck his hand in his left pocket, wiggled it into the sock and ran his fingers over the forked tongue, just to make sure he hadn't mixed up the pockets. Then he said, 'And if I give you the figurine I have in my pocket—the one I'm holding right now—you'll tell me who my parents are? And help us find a less harmful way to stop the tunnel?' He thought for a moment. What else would Saga ask for? 'And give us protection?'

'Yes, yes. If you insist, we will even protect your little friend.'

'Do you promise?' Alfred could almost hear Saga's voice like an alarm bell in his head. He was about to trick a faerie. And not just any faerie—someone who was most likely a close ally of the queen.

Amanita narrowed her eyes. Her frown made the living hair clips scramble to hold on. 'And then you give it to me willingly?' she asked.

'Yes.' Alfred held his breath.

'I promise,' Amanita said.

At that exact moment, Saga screamed.

25

Shadow Thieves

Another scream reverberated through the trees, followed by Saga's calls for help.

Alfred's hand, still in his pocket, clutched the fork-tongued carving. He stared up at Amanita, but she pretended not to hear the screams. He waited two heartbeats, hoping she would tell him about his parents fast, but he couldn't let Saga down.

'We have to help her.' He turned away and set off.

'And the truth about your ancestry?' Amanita called after him.

'In a minute!' he yelled, pelting up the path. He hadn't realized how far they'd walked. With every stride, the words 'faerie blood' pounded in his head.

When he reached the clearing by the sinkhole, the sun peeked out between clouds. Saga was sitting on a tree stump nearby with her head in her hands. She appeared to be unharmed, so why had she screamed at the worst possible moment?

'What's wrong?' He panted, leaning forward to catch his breath, ignoring the throbbing pain in his left knee.

Saga stared straight ahead, wiping at her eyes, smudging her tear-streaked cheeks. 'Look!' she said.

Alfred's eyes swept over the undergrowth, trying to spot some kind of animal that could've bitten her. The tall trees cast shadow columns on the uneven ground and the carpet of toadstools. Nothing seemed out of place. He felt a touch of resentment that she'd prevented him from finally getting answers.

She stood up. 'The-there,' she hiccupped.

His gaze followed her finger down, and then he saw it. In front of himself, his shadow stretched away from his feet. In front of Saga...

Nothing. She had no shadow.

'They—the little people... I saw them. They stole my shadow.'

'Let's get back to Amanita. She can probably—'

'No. Wait. I think she had something to do with it.'

'That's ridiculous. She was with me.'

'Yes, but when you left, one of her butterfly hair clips took off from the back of her head. I was staring at it and holding my hand out towards it. I didn't like that she had them in her hair—'

'Me neither,' Alfred muttered.

'I thought perhaps I could help it. It fluttered towards me in wide circles. It was kind of colourless and hard to see against the trees—perhaps it was more of a faerie moth. I kept watching it. Its circles became smaller the closer it came. And suddenly I was just so tired. I sat down on the tree stump, and I think the moth landed on my hair.'

Alfred walked round her, peering behind her ginger buns. 'It's not there now,' he said, wondering if Saga was mistaken. The butterfly faeries he'd seen in Amanita's hair had all been blue.

'I must've fallen asleep, but I woke up and saw them. The little people. Little Father was rolling up my shadow, and Little Mother was clipping it away with silver scissors that were almost as big as she was herself. And I could understand what they were saying. They were going on and on about Her letting them have the scissors. Little Mother kept adjusting her pinny and asking Little Father whether he thought she could cut a snippet off for themselves. She wanted to use it as a curtain on sunny days. My shadow! As a curtain!'

Alfred remembered the pixies chattering about scissors. Was this what they'd been planning all along?

'At first, I thought I was dreaming. It was so unreal, seeing my shadow being rolled up like an old sleeping bag. But then my leg began burning, and I saw it was right in that patch of nettles. I pinched my arm, and it hurt, and that's when I screamed. But it was too late. They ran away with my shadow.'

'They thought you led the diggers to the Faerie Hill... Where did they go?'

Saga pointed at the sinkhole. 'They jumped,' she said, 'Like Mr Tumbleweed. Isn't it strange though that I can see and hear the faeries now that he has left me? Perhaps, all these years, he was preventing me from seeing them. Perhaps he wasn't my friend at all.'

'Or perhaps he was protecting you. You've been running around in the woods, and nothing has ever happened to you until now that he isn't here. Perhaps the faeries haven't been able to see you either.'

Saga frowned. 'Amanita did call me the invisible girl...'

'Come on,' Alfred said. 'She promised to help us find a solution and she offered us protection. That must include getting your shadow back. And she told me I have faerie blood, so you were right—I am a changeling.' He began walking before he could see Saga's expression.

While they hurried down the path, he told her about the deal he'd made with Amanita.

'This is not good,' Saga said. 'Why did you have to trick her?'

'I didn't want to lose the water-sprite figurine.'

'I know. But you don't think she suspects anything, do you?'

Alfred shook his head. 'I have a feeling she really wants to help. But there are these rules she must follow.'

'Hmmm... I just don't think we can trust her. She's a faerie.'

'I don't trust her blindly,' Alfred said, getting a little annoyed again. Saga might think she knew a lot about faeries, but he was the one they recognized and chose to talk to. By now he had more actual experience in dealing with faeries than she did, if he discounted Mr Tumbleweed. Besides, Amanita had said he had faerie blood. And why would she trick another faerie? 'Have you forgotten that I'm a changeling, so I'm a faerie too?'

Saga didn't answer.

When they arrived at the spot where Alfred had left her, Amanita was gone. He called her name again and again, growing more and more frantic. She didn't reappear.

'She must have gone back to the faerie realm. We'll go after her.' He'd been so close to learning the truth. As if his legs didn't hurt and his feet weren't sore, he hurried back towards the sinkhole.

'It's too dangerous,' Saga called from behind.

'You don't have to worry. I'm the one who tried to trick her. Not the other way around.'

'But without Mr Tumbleweed, without my shadow... With those little people out to get us...'

'I have to find her.' Whatever Saga said didn't matter.

His heart pounded. The racing blood sounded like the ocean in his ears. Above this distant rumbling, the voice in his head repeated over and over again, 'faerie blood.'

'Wait!'

He stopped on the path and turned, yelling, 'I just want to know who I am! Is that too much to ask?'

Saga didn't flinch. She stepped right up to him and put both hands on his shoulders. 'Nobody can tell you that,' she said quietly. 'You decide who you want to be.'

He took a deep, rattling breath. 'But who is that?'

She studied him, saying, 'To me, you're someone who is helpful and doesn't judge others, even if their hairdo looks weird. You're a person who wants to help save nature. You also happen to be able to see and talk to faeries, which is interesting, but not the reason I want you as my friend.'

'Even if I'm not even a person?'

'Of course you're a person.'

'I still have to talk to Amanita. I have to know *what* I am,' he said, his voice almost calm. 'You don't have to come.' He set off again, muttering, 'And I must find another way to stop that tunnel. Those poisonous vines can't stay.'

Saga was right. It would be dangerous. Amanita had told him so too, and he didn't fancy meeting the little people on their home turf. He also still feared what would happen if he found his faerie parents. But he had to face that fear head-on.

Alfred wished Saga would go with him, but he was prepared to go alone. If the creeping vines were less resistant than Amanita thought and the drilling ruined the entrance to Faerie, he might never get another opportunity.

Even worse, if the plants really were deadly, Dad was in danger.

26

Into the Sinkhole

Alfred reached the sinkhole and picked up the rope. The jerking vines rustled. Inside his head, the voice kept repeating, 'faerie blood.'

He didn't hear Saga until she stood next to him, taking the coils out of his hands.

'Of course I'm coming with you,' she said, and tied two rope ends together with a sturdy knot. At home, she'd already made knots along the rope at regular intervals. 'You can't go into Faerie on your own.'

'Thank you,' he said, and, for a moment, the voice in his head stopped chanting.

'We have to find a way to stop the tunnel project, without harming anyone—faerie, human, animal—or anything else in nature. And this might be our only chance. Plus, you need me. I've packed lots of useful things. Like these.' She held out two pairs of gardening gloves.

After they had fastened the rope to the steel rings, Saga tied her shoulder bag to its other end, and they lowered the bag into the sinkhole. The coils unspooled until the bag landed on the surface far below.

'Thirty metres is like a ten-storey building,' Alfred said.

'I wish I'd been able to find climbing harnesses.' Saga swung one leg over the fence.

'Let me go first. You're much better at climbing...'

'If you're sure?' She stood aside.

'Yeah.' He didn't want to pull Saga with him if he fell. Besides, he might not even get hurt if that happened. Perhaps he'd just bounce back up like Mr Tumbleweed. At least, that was what he told himself while he climbed down. Perhaps it helped, because he made it all the way.

Alfred put the gloves in a back pocket and stood rubbing his hands, watching Saga descend. Despite the gloves, after sliding between the knots, his palms were sore and his fingers stiff.

'We made it,' she said, when she too landed on the mossy ground.

'*It, it, it,*' the bare domed walls behind them echoed.

Alfred looked up at the small opening to the sky. He couldn't imagine how he would be able to climb back up.

'Mr Tumbleweed,' Saga called.

The only answer was the echoed '*Weed, weed, weed...*'

'He went in there.' Alfred pointed to the part of the cavern that was entirely overgrown.

Here, vines slithered out of the moss and climbed the walls. The creepers criss-crossed in the air, weaving a loose-masked net. Above them, the net tightened into a dense green curtain and flowed out of the sinkhole.

On their way to this area of the cavern, Saga and Alfred circled boulders and small trees, looking for anything that could be an entrance to somewhere else. They were following the net of plants, searching for a path through to the wall, when Alfred stumbled.

Instinctively, he grabbed hold of the nearest vine just as he remembered he'd taken his gloves off. The vine snapped in two. He tumbled to the ground, tearing a large hole in the net, landing entangled in creepers. A pile of the purple-veined leaves cushioned his cheek.

He scrambled back up, and stood staring at his hands and arms, waiting for the redness and the stinging, burning sensation Saga had described.

He felt nothing. No rash appeared.

'Must be my faerie blood,' he muttered. 'Wait here.' Pushing his way in through the curtain, tearing at the plants, he made it to the wall. All around him, the vines continued to jerk upwards. Their coordination was almost perfect. Except...

In a spot just above his head, the leaves fluttered between the jerks. The cliff wall behind them appeared to be darker.

After grabbing an armful of the creepers, Alfred dragged them aside, revealing a deep cleft in the rock.

'I think I've found something. Wait there!'

'*Heir, heir, heir,*' the echo replied.

But Saga came barging through the almost-path he'd made. She had a scarf over her head and upper body, as if she were dressed up as a ghost. She obviously couldn't see much, because he had to stop her before she collided with the wall.

'I'll go first.' He used the vines to pull himself up. His arms and shoulders were strong from swimming, and he found small ledges to place his feet.

When he reached the hole in the wall, he swung through the remaining creepers, landing on his knees. The vines snapped back to cover the gap. Only weak light seeped in between their leaves.

He got up—there was just room to stand—and pulled part of the plant curtain aside. With the light from the sinkhole, he could see further into the darkness.

'It's a tunnel,' he said, and bundled the vines together on both sides of the tunnel mouth. Then, lying on his stomach, stretching his arms down, he pulled Saga up. He tried his best to keep her away from the poisonous creepers. Afterwards, though, she stood rubbing her itching wrists where gaps had appeared between her long-sleeved top and the gardening gloves.

She sniffed.

'Is it very painful?'

Saga shrugged and asked, 'D'you think this is where the little people went with my shadow? And Mr Tumbleweed?'

'Yeah.' He didn't quite know if it was the rash or her missing shadow or the thought of the tree sprite that made her sniff.

'I can't believe he just left me.'

Alfred pointed his phone's flashlight to the ground. There were no visible tracks on the pale hard stone.

'Let's see where this leads,' he said.

But it was not long before the tunnel divided into three.

'Which way?'

'I don't know.' Saga sniffed again. 'What if he never comes back, then I'm just... ordinary.'

Alfred recalled the triumphant smile on the little creature's face when he'd spoken those last word. There was a finality to the statement that he didn't think Saga had understood from his translation. 'Try to picture where we would be above ground,' he said, instead of answering.

Saga took her notebook out and opened it to the map with *SINKHOLE* in the top corner.

'You said the ivy was crawling back in the direction we came from. Is that this way?' Alfred pointed to one of the paths on her map.

'No. The public caves are somewhere far over there.' Saga turned her notebook forty-five degrees. In the light from the phone, the red welts on her wrists shone. 'I think we should go in the opposite direction. That way.' She pointed at the leftmost passage.

Without hesitation, Alfred stepped past her into the dark tunnel.

27

The Haze in the Labyrinth

'Wait!' Saga extracted a wood-encased hourglass and hung it from a belt loop using a carabiner. We can't lose track of time. It's 12.25 now.' She pointed to the top of the hourglass. 'I'll add a chalk mark every half hour, when I turn it.'

'But I have this.' Alfred waved his phone in front of her face.

'And you're sure that'll work where we're going?' She stuffed the notebook in her shoulder bag and took out a flashlight and a ball of yarn. Turquoise yarn with a crochet needle sticking out.

Alfred reached out to touch the thread. He knew this exact colour.

'I got it from your granny. Ages ago. I'm making a hat,' she said, unravelling the circle she'd crocheted. 'But that can wait. We need a trail of breadcrumbs.' She'd stopped sniffing. Having something concrete to do seemed to have cheered her up.

Before they headed into the tunnel, Saga tied a snippet of yarn round a loose stone, marking their path. They followed the left-hand wall, lit up by Alfred's phone light, until they came to another intersection. Here, Saga bit off a length of yarn and tied it round another stone, before they again took the tunnel on the left. It snaked its way through the hill, never going straight but curving, mainly left. Sometimes there were scattered rocks on the floor that they had to climb over, and sometimes the passage became so narrow they had to squeeze sideways though a gap.

'Perhaps we need to go right next time,' Saga said.

But that wasn't possible. At the next fork, a rockfall blocked off the right-hand tunnel. Some of the stones were small, but they wouldn't be able to move the larger rocks. There was no telling when the ceiling had collapsed. Alfred wondered if it could've happened twelve years ago, when Nereida disappeared.

After a while, the tunnel ahead brightened. At the next intersection, scattered weak daylight from a side tunnel dotted the ground. Without pausing, Alfred ran towards the light. At the end of the short tunnel, the rays twinkled through a curtain of leaves. Upon reaching it, he tore the plants aside and looked into... the bottom of the sinkhole.

'We've been walking in a circle,' Saga said behind him. When he turned, she picked up a stone, dangling it by its turquoise thread. The very first stone she had placed.

Saga turned the hourglass and drew the first chalk mark. Their loop had taken half an hour. They shared a cereal bar and took turns drinking from Saga's water bottle, before setting off again.

This time, they chose the centre tunnel. It led straight away from the sinkhole. They walked for a long time, Saga in front, without coming upon any side tunnels. The ground was smooth and shone in the flashlight. Sharp rocks stuck out from the walls and ceiling, creating angular shadowy shapes.

Alfred wondered if they were getting closer to an entrance to Faerie. He tried to imagine that other realm. Would it be a fairy-tale world full of colour? Perhaps there would be Tinker Bell-like faeries flittering about, spreading magical glitter over everything. Or perhaps not quite... Not if the world was populated by grumpy tree sprites and vicious pixies.

Without warning, Saga stopped. The tunnel ended abruptly at a wall of rock.

'A dead end,' he said.

Saga ran her hand down over the wall. 'This isn't natural. It's as smooth as polished marble.' She shoved with both hands. 'Perhaps it will open if we knock in a pattern or pull a lever somewhere...'

A faint tune came through the wall. 'Sh...' Alfred strained his ears. 'Can you hear that?'

'What?'

'Music!'

She shook her head.

Without touching it, Alfred stepped right up to the wall and shone the light from his phone over the gleaming surface. Saga was right, it really didn't seem natural. The music became clearer. He could hear the song too. The voices beckoned him closer.

'How?' he muttered to himself.

'Just push, push, push,' the voices sang. But it couldn't be that easy.

He thrust the phone into his back pocket, placed both palms on the smooth surface and pushed.

His hands met no resistance. The wall dissolved into a charcoal-coloured mist.

'How on earth...' Saga held onto his arm as they walked into the haze. 'My glasses are fogging up,' she said. 'I can't see a thing.'

For a second, her flashlight lit up millions of microscopic particles. Then it went out.

Impenetrable darkness surrounded them. Alfred couldn't even see his own hands. Saga gripped his arm harder. He fumbled to light the screen on his phone, but it was dead, although the battery had been fully charged. Still, he wasn't scared, because he could hear the music.

The charcoal haze fell like fine cooling sprays on his skin. Saga's hand on his arm felt warm and comforting. He put one foot in front of the other, not shifting his weight forward until he found solid ground under his shoe, walking towards a song of, *'Come, come, come.'*

Gradually, the haze brightened. Through small gaps in the ceiling far above, cones of light turned the mist into glitter. They emerged in a cave.

The lyrics changed seamlessly to a chant of, *'Welcome, welcome, welcome.'*

Saga let go of him to wipe her glasses as they walked towards the centre of the space. Here, a deep crevice cut straight across the floor. The gap was so narrow they could step over it. At the bottom, far below, an underground stream rushed. It sent up the spray that became the misty glitter.

The stream itself cast prisms of silvery light up on the cave ceiling. The water was so far down, Alfred could hardly see it. But the song that had been guiding him came from the depths. The unseen choir was still stuck on, *'Welcome.'*

After they'd crossed the crevice, he stood on the edge and tried to spot the threads of the stream through the mist. He longed to jump into the current. While he listened to its sweet sounds, he became aware of the way the water rushed over the rocks it had spent millennia forming. He could sense how the smooth ripples softened the hard surface. It was mesmerizing.

'That's the spring that comes out in Granny's shed,' he whispered to himself. Then realized that it was also the stream that had delivered his shoes.

'How can you tell?' Saga asked.

'What?' Alfred shook his head, coming out of the daze.

'How can you tell that this stream leads to your granny's? You just said.'

Alfred listened to the music. The greenish-blue notes sounded extra clear. 'I don't know. I just can.'

'We can test it.' Saga tore off a snippet of yarn.

'No!' he said, but it was too late. She'd already dropped it into the opening.

The moment the snippet landed, the stream lit up the cave in a turquoise light show. Alfred saw the individual threads reflected in all their blue and green colours. It was the most beautiful sight he'd ever seen.

Then long slimy tendrils shot out of the water, reaching for them, lashing through the space around them with loud whip-cracks.

'Run!' he yelled.

28

Dripstone Caverns and Creatures

They sprinted away from the crevice in the ground. The water sprite's hair lashed out after them. To evade the strands, they ran towards the darkest corner of the cave.

'Over here,' Saga called.

Alfred saw the mouth of a tunnel, as one slimy tendril tightened round his arm. He continued to run while he tore at the bindings. From that single strand he knew her. Knew it was the same water sprite. Lillith. And he knew she would've recognized him too.

With a last hard tug, he freed himself.

Escaping, Alfred followed Saga into the new tunnel. A shriek echoed behind them.

At full pelt, they ran until they were far away from the cave, only stopping to breathe when they reached a fork. To the left, a tunnel went steeply downhill. To the right, rough steps cut into the rock were going up.

'Up!' They both said at the same time.

While Saga tied yarn round two stones and placed them on the ground, Alfred stretched a cramping muscle and made circles with his right foot. It was only now he noticed the light.

Saga's flashlight and his phone had died, but somehow there was still light enough to see by. Just above their heads, millions of glow worms lit up the tunnel. Like tiny fairy lights, they hung on gossamer threads. And they were swaying.

'There's a draught from the lower tunnel,' he said.

'Okay, let's go that way then.' Saga moved one of the yarn-encircled stones she'd just placed to mark their new path.

They had walked for a couple of minutes when the passage opened up into an enormous cavern.

It was dimmer here than in the tunnel. The worms glowed far above. In a few places, pale light fell in through thin cracks to the outside world. Gigantic stalagmite statues reached up towards the high vaulted ceiling. They were met by icicle-like stalactites.

It was magnificent.

'Wow!' Alfred tried to gauge the size of the cavern.

'I've lost my sense of direction completely...' Saga said. 'I could've sworn the public caves were in the opposite direction. And this is so much more impressive than I remem—'

'It's at least five Olympic-sized pools long. That's 250 metres!'

'This isn't one of the public caves. They have signposts, and there's a raised walkway all the way round, with a fence so you can't touch the dripstones. And this cave is much, much bigger than any of them. Perhaps my sense of direction isn't bad after all.'

They made their way down through the imposing shadowy formations, taking turns to point out spectacular dripstones. Some twirled upwards like oversized candles. Others hung in groups of downward pointing spears or had merged into wavy stone curtains. Coral-like shapes bloomed between the massive columns that appeared to support the arched ceiling.

At the far end, the ground was much lower than where they'd come out of the tunnel. The cracks that let in light were high above now. Directly underneath one of the cracks, a stalagmite had snapped clean in half. The broken-off part lay in three pieces among crumbled stones, next to a smashed yellow plastic box.

'What's that doing here?' Saga picked the box up and turned it to look at all sides. 'What is it?'

'A theodolite,' Alfred said. Dad usually had one in the car. 'Engineers use them to measure angles. For road constructions. And tunnels.'

Saga's eyes lit up. 'I overheard my dad and uncle talking about one of the engineers they recovered this week. He'd mumbled about a dripstone cave. But everyone thinks he's lost his mind because the caves are on the other side of the hill. What if he fell down here? Perhaps we're near the building site!'

'But they found him in a sinkhole, didn't they?'

'Yes, somewhere further uphill.'

'I don't understand,' Alfred said. 'Is this Faerie or the real world?' He'd thought they were in the faerie realm after they passed through the rock wall and the strange mist. Were they in a passage between the worlds? Or was all of Faerie just underground tunnels and caves?

Saga just shook her head sadly. 'If we're anywhere near the building site, this natural wonder will be destroyed when they start drilling.'

They spent some time walking along the walls of the enormous cavern, searching for gaps and tunnels, but there were none. Without further discussion, they made their way back into the tunnel they had come from. At the crossroads, they continued up the rough steps.

Now that they were on stairs, Alfred felt the strain in his legs again. He was beginning to wonder if they'd ever find a way out of the underground, when they arrived at another dripstone cavern.

Devoid of glow worms, it was darker than the first cavern. The ceiling was lower. Many of the nearby stalagmites grew together with stalactites, creating solid pillars—some monumental columns, others thin prison bars.

Ethereal silvery light shimmered through a wide opening on the opposite side of the cavern. Despite this light, shadows hugged the formations. The still, musty air whiffed of mould and decay. Like a thick cape, it wrapped the dripstones in a gloomy silence.

They tiptoed round the first stalagmite column, its base like that of an ancient oak. On the other side, they saw the sculptures.

Small creature sculptures covered the cavern floor. Large animals—bears and boars and wolves—stood frozen amidst mice and martens and squirrels. Owls and eagles spread their wings next to the butterflies and moths. Icicle formations, dripped down over centuries, pinned some of them to the ground with their pointy tips.

The sculptures resembled Granny's creature carvings. All were as finely whittled as hers. All, no matter what animal they depicted, were the same size as hers. And, just like hers, they were all somehow alive.

In combination with the otherworldly light, the strangely charged atmosphere convinced Alfred that they were now definitely in another realm.

Beside a carved butterfly, he caught sight of a small movement. Wings fluttered. At first he thought he'd imagined it, like he so often did at Granny's cottage, but then he saw the glints of colour.

'Over there,' he whispered and pointed.

A tiny, winged creature, like Amanita's hair clips, fluttered round a cat-sized, carved butterfly. It landed on an antenna, before flitting to a wingtip.

Gingerly, to avoid tripping over any of the figures, they walked closer. Crouching by the butterfly, which seemed to be made of wood, just like Granny's carvings, they studied the little faerie.

It had orange cropped hair. Wings in the same luminous orange sported a brown web-like pattern and bright white spots. A flood of tears ran from its large eyes and merged with snot from the pointed, beak-like nose. From its tiny mouth came loud heartbreaking wails.

Although they were so close they could touch it, the faerie was completely oblivious to their presence.

29

The Duke of Burgundy

'What's the matter?' Alfred asked softly.

The little faerie dived down behind the carved butterfly. It peeked out between the front and back wing, still sobbing uncontrollably.

Saga took a tissue out of her shoulder bag and peeled the layers apart. After tearing a corner off, she offered it to the faerie.

It blew its nose, with a sound that was impossibly loud for such a small thing.

'It's my... my... Holly Blue,' it hiccupped. 'It's all my... my fault, but I did tell them they shou-shouldn't—' A tearful shudder went through the little creature.

'What's wrong with your, er, blue holly?' Alfred asked.

'It's obvious, isn't it? Everything's wrong!' The orange butterfly-faerie sobbed, rising into the air.

'I'm sorry, but I don't even know what a blue holly is,' Alfred said.

'Holly is a plant with red berries. But I've never seen one that's blue.' Saga handed the faerie another torn-off corner of the tissue.

'Holly Blue! And they're not a plant. They are my bestest—'

The faerie blew its nose. 'Best friend. And I told them all the fame in the realm wasn't worth the risk. But they wouldn't listen.'

'Why don't you go back and start at the beginning.' Alfred sat down on the floor of the cave, sighing with relief at getting off his feet.

The little faerie took a deep ragged breath. 'I'm the Duke of Burgundy, and I was born on a warm summer's night underneath the leaf of a primrose in the royal gardens.'

'Maybe not that far back,' said Alfred as the same time as Saga asked, 'The Duke of Burgundy?'

'You can call me Duke. That's what my friend—' The Duke of Burgundy exploded in another sob. 'It's just... Holly Blue has been my bestest friend ever since we hatched. Back when we still had sunshine and daylight.'

'But what happened to her?' Alfred asked.

'Not her. Them,' Duke said. 'They were a born musician. Every deserted spiderweb became their instrument.'

'Didn't they ever get stuck, or caught by a spider?'

'Not Holly Blue. Not ever. They were too nimble. And the spiders like music. Lacy even spun them a lyre between two rose thorns. I wish she hadn't, because that's when things started going wrong.'

'What happened?' Alfred said again.

'She heard Holly Blue play.'

'Who?' asked Saga. 'Lacy?'

'No. Come closer.'

They both leant so close to the Duke of Burgundy that Alfred could feel the fluttering of wings on his nose.

The faerie looked left and right before whispering, 'The queen.'

'The queen?' Saga repeated. 'The faerie queen?'

'We've heard about her,' Alfred muttered.

'Shhh!' The Duke of Burgundy flew up in the air and turned in a slow circle. 'Don't talk about her,' he whispered, when he landed on the back of the wooden butterfly.

Alfred's eyes swept over the surrounding sculptures, searching for forked tongues. He patted the lump in his pocket. He wished he could get rid of the spy. Perhaps he should leave it here, hidden in plain sight among the woodcarvings, until he found Amanita. Though he doubted Duke would like that.

'So what happened?' Saga asked. 'Didn't the quee... er... Didn't She like Holly Blue's music?'

'Oh, She loved it! That was the problem. She wanted Holly Blue to play in the finest ballroom at the fortress. She wanted them to play the eternal dance. Holly Blue was ever so flattered. Normally our kind are not asked to do important things. Because, well, it's... We're easily distracted. And, you know, the eternal dance—it goes on for ever. Literally for ever.'

Alfred could see how that would cause problems for an easily distracted faerie.

'For ever is a long time. No one dares to suggest She shortens for ever.' Duke blew his nose. 'It's an unbearably long time not to see your bestest friend. It's an unbearably long time not to sort of fly up to one of the windows to look at your friend, when you can hear their music all the way down under the primroses in the garden. And when you have then watched your friend play for an eternity, it's impossible not to tap the window just once to make them look up...'

'So you knocked, and they saw you and hit a wrong note. Is that it?' Saga asked.

The Duke of Burgundy put his tiny face in his tiny hands. 'It's worse,' he mumbled. He looked up at them through tear-laced eyelashes. 'Holly Blue was so excited to see me that they stopped playing altogether and flew to the window. I signalled to them to get back to the lyre, and that's what they did, but the dancers had stopped dancing. It was only for a moment, but it was enough for the two new humans to come to their senses.'

'The eternal dance is actually real!' Saga said. 'D'you think those new humans could be the engineers?'

Alfred shrugged. He wasn't interested in the engineers. 'But there are other humans, right? Some of them must've been in the ballrooms much longer.'

'Oh, yes. Some have been dancing since the beginning of for ever.'

Before Alfred could ask about those dancers, Saga said, 'What did the... What did She do to Holly Blue?'

'She did what She always does when She's displeased. She imprisoned the essence of Holly Blue.' The Duke of Burgundy sank down until he lay on the wood-carved butterfly with his arms round its neck. 'She imprisoned their spirit!'

'Maybe we can help you find and free this spirit...'

'No one except She can free a spirit. And as for finding it, I thought that was clear.' The Duke of Burgundy looked up at Alfred with a frown. 'It's here,' he said and stroked the wooden butterfly. 'It's right here.'

'You mean—' Alfred began.

'That butterfly is Holly Blue?' Saga finished.

'No. You don't understand. This butterfly is the prison for their essence. Just like all the others.'

Around them stood hundreds—no, thousands—of wood-carvings. Alfred's fingers touched the little water-sprite figurine in his pocket. They were prisons. Every single one of the wooden figures held a captured spirit.

'This wasn't in any of the fairy tales I've read,' Saga muttered. 'How do you know that one's Holly Blue?'

The other carved butterflies showed only tiny differences in the shape of their wings, the angle of their antennae or the knots in the wood.

'I can feel it,' the Duke of Burgundy said. 'I can feel their spirit.'

'May I?' Alfred reached out and let his hand hover over the small sculpture. The Duke of Burgundy slid down, and now Alfred could sense the tiny vibrations in the surrounding air—the essence of Holly Blue. A current pulsed, like in the air around the little mole in his room at Granny's cottage.

'If you don't mind, I'd like to be alone with Holly Blue,' Duke said.

'Perhaps we could carry their prison outside in the garden for you,' Saga suggested.

'No, no, no, no.' The tiny faerie shook his head violently. 'They have to stay here. That's their only chance. They must be in this cavern for the birthday honours. On Her birthday, She usually pardons a random number of random spirits.'

'When's her birthday?' Saga asked.

'It used to be once in a blue moon...'

'What? Like when there are two full moons in a month?'

He nodded. 'But that doesn't work any more—you'll see.'

'Are there human spirits here too?' The woodcarvings Alfred could see were all shaped like animals.

'Oh no,' the Duke of Burgundy said. 'They are all up in the ballrooms.'

'How do we get out of here? Through the opening back there?' Alfred pointed at the hole in the cave wall that admitted the silvery light.

'No, no, no, no, Her spy is over there.' The Duke of Burgundy explained how they could take a side tunnel that came out in the forest. 'Now, if you don't mind...' His face contorted again.

Before they left the little faerie, Saga stacked torn-up layers of the tissue in a neat pile by Holly Blue's prison.

They walked like a funeral procession through the graveyard of wood-carved creatures. Now that Alfred knew what each of the sculptures represented, the atmosphere seemed even more hushed and solemn.

His eyes roamed over them, searching for figures with forked tongues, prepared to duck or run at the sight of a spy. Nearer the opening to the silvery light, they found the side tunnel behind a long row of stalactites. But something about the ethereal glow drew him closer.

'Wait here, I'm just going to peek outside,' Alfred said. He sneaked forward, careful not to make any sound. He was thinking about merging with the background, although he wasn't convinced his invisibility trick worked on faeries.

The opening was a little higher up than he had thought. He would have to heave himself up to look out. Before doing so, he glanced back to where Saga stood, and that's when he saw it.

Right behind him, facing the opening, was an enormous stalagmite. It was shaped like a long face, with dark empty holes for eyes and a horizontal slit for a mouth.

Was that the spy?

Alfred tried to still his racing heart and slow his breath.

The slit on the stalagmite opened into a gaping mouth.

Ever so lightly, he tiptoed back towards Saga. From where she waited, she couldn't see the spy, but he knew she could see the panic in his eyes. He was still at least ten steps in front of the spy. After putting a finger to his lips, signalling for her to be quiet, he waved her away with his hands.

Silently, she disappeared into the side tunnel.

Inching forward, he passed the dripstone statue, just as a forked tongue the length of his arm slithered out of its mouth.

Alfred froze.

With a deep rumble, the stalagmite rotated to face him. The tongue flicked, reaching for him.

Trying to get away, he flattened himself against the cavern wall.

The tongue grew longer. One of the forked tips brushed over the back of his hand. Instantly, glaring eyes filled the empty eye sockets.

Abandoning all efforts to stay calm, Alfred pushed off from the wall and ran.

Like a siren, the stalagmite spy began to wail.

30

The Moonlit Forest

With the siren from the queen's spy ringing in his ears, Alfred hurtled after Saga. He zigzagged between the woodcarvings. A few toppled over.

The wailing sounded like screeches from attacking birds of prey. It chased him into the side tunnel.

Saga was waiting, where the tunnel became a long staircase, carved into the limestone. Wall-mounted, silvery-glowing torches cast dim light on the uneven steps that led up and out of the underground. The spy still wailed behind them.

'Go,' Alfred said, although the cramp in his leg had worsened after sitting down. With every step, a jab from the sore tendons ran up his calf. He lagged behind Saga, as she sped up the stairs.

Somewhere above them, a river rushed. To take his mind off the pain, he tried to catch its music through the wails and the rock. He couldn't help wondering if it fed the stream in the cave below, if it fed Granny's spring, if it was Lillith's home.

The staircase ended at the bottom of a shallow hole in the ground. As they were climbing out of the hole, the siren noise stopped.

They emerged in a forest. A dark moonlit forest.

Trying to slow his breath, Alfred inhaled. The air was cool and damp and a touch mouldy. A grey mist clung to the trees. Moonlight cast long dark shadows. Long dark shadows in two directions. In the sky above the tree crowns, two full moons shone. It felt as if they were pulling at him in a tug of war.

'Faerie is not at all what I expected,' Saga said. 'I'd thought nature would be healthy here, you know, without humans to destroy everything. But it's like this forest is ill and needs fresh air and sunshine.'

Ignoring his cramping leg, Alfred revolved slowly, taking in the surroundings.

Moss and lichen covered the ground and crept over fallen branches and rotten tree stumps. Boulders had been turned into green globes. Toadstools dotted everything with red splashes, like boils. And the ivy-like creepers climbed up every tree in sight, covering their fungus-infected trunks.

This sinister place was nothing like the fairy-tale world he'd imagined either.

As he turned, a smell of decay wafted up from the undergrowth. His two faint shadows swirled around his feet. He noticed Saga staring at them.

'How long were we in the tunnels?' he asked quietly. If it was evening, Granny would be worried.

Saga held up her hourglass. The sand was halfway through and there were four chalk marks at the top. 'It's only been two hours and about fifteen minutes.'

'Should I call Amanita?' He wanted to seal the deal he'd made with her—information and protection and a chance to find a solution to the tunnel problem without the deadly plants in exchange for the fork-tongued figurine. It seemed an unfair bargain from her perspective. He longed for the information about his parents, and the protection she'd offered might be imminently needed in this scary place. Whereas he was so desperate to get rid of the spy figurine, he would've happily handed it over without getting anything in return.

'I really don't trust her,' Saga said. 'Those butterfly faeries she had in her hair... They must've been scared of her. And there's something else I've remembered...' Saga crouched by a ring of white-spotted red toadstools. 'You know what these are called?'

'Fly mushrooms?'

'Their scientific name is Amanita something. I think most toxic mushrooms are in the Amanita family. That's where I'd heard her name before.'

'Are you saying she's poisonous?'

'I don't know. But don't ever eat anything she's offering.'

'It's just a name.'

'Didn't I tell you names have power? Let's look around and see if we can find some friendly faeries.' She walked to a nearby gap in the trees. 'Come,' she called softly. 'You've got to see this.'

From where she stood, they could see the ancient extinct volcano. Except it wasn't a hill any more, but a cone-shaped fortress that rose from the forest. Alfred counted more than twenty storeys. Silvery light gleamed from the windows on the top floors. The others were dark and reflected the two moons.

'Listen.' Faint, exquisite music—harps and flutes and something else he couldn't quite place—came from the fortress. The soft tones were enticing. It had to be the music of the eternal dance. 'You hear that?'

Saga nodded.

They stood in silence for a while, listening to the distant music. Was this where his mother was? No, not his mother. Nereida. Dancing on an eternal loop, with no sense of time and place. Could he free her from the spell and find answers? Perhaps even bring her back to Dad...

Next to him, Saga swayed, her eyes unfocused. One of her feet bobbed up and down. When Alfred glanced at the hourglass that hung from her belt, the sand had run out. He didn't feel affected by the music, but the thought that they could've been standing there for hours made his body tense up.

He elbowed her. 'You need to turn that.'

'Oh,' she said and blinked a few times. She stared down at her bobbing toes. 'This is not good.' After adding a chalk line, she turned the hourglass. 'I'm sure Mr Tumbleweed will be at the fortress. He likes music. Except when I used to play the recorder. He always screwed his face up and put his stick-fingers into the knots on the sides of his head.'

She took a pair of pink fluffy earmuffs out of her shoulder bag. On them, sequinned rainbows glittered. 'Luckily, I brought these in case the faerie music really was as mesmerizing as some stories claim. I also have some earplugs for you, but apparently you don't need any,' she added, before putting her earmuffs on. 'There must be other faeries we can talk to up there. And perhaps if I find Mr Tumbleweed. If he really has protected me all these years...' Her voice wobbled. 'I think... I hope, he'll help us and come home with me.'

Alfred doubted they could expect any help from the tree sprite, but she had put the earmuffs on, so he just nodded. Although he feared they were being lured into a trap, he followed Saga towards the fortress.

As they walked, he startled at every sound that wasn't the music. Glancing around, he tried to spot anything that looked like one of the queen's spies. To see if they were being followed, he kept looking over his shoulder. That was what he was doing when Saga suddenly grabbed hold of him.

'Watch where you're going,' she yelled, much too loud in the quiet forest.

In front of them, a ravine had appeared. Rushing tones from its depth mingled with the eternal music. Unlike the crevice in the underground cave, they couldn't just jump over this gap. It was several metres wide and ran as far as Alfred could see in both directions, blocking off their path to the faerie fortress.

After a silent discussion with their hands, they turned right and walked uphill along the ravine. Before long, this path also ended in a vertical drop. They stood atop a limestone wall that was even higher than the one behind Granny's cottage. From here, they could see far out over the open country to another of the extinct volcanos. Light from a bonfire flickered at its top.

Although the two moons shone on the flat area between them and the other volcano, they couldn't make out any details of the scenery. An odd emptiness absorbed the moonlight. It shrouded the vast plain, obscuring all contours of the colourless landscape.

Saga turned the hourglass and drew a chalk mark, before taking her notebook out. She wrote something down and showed him the page. It was one of her maps—a real map she'd glued in. 'We're here', she'd written with an arrow pointing to a clifftop, marked as a scenic viewpoint. Below the limestone wall, in the real world, the roads of a city criss-crossed the map. Here, in the faerie realm, all they could see from the viewpoint was the strangely empty space.

Saga tugged at Alfred's T-shirt and whispered, 'A stag.' She pointed along the ridge, a short distance from where they stood. The silhouette of three-pronged antlers stood out in the silvery light.

But it wasn't a stag.

Below the antlers, the outline of the creature resembled a large dog rather than a deer.

It turned in their direction.

Alfred gripped Saga's arm. He held her in place while he exhaled, signalling with a slow downward hand movement that she should stay calm. He tried to slow his breath and his pulse, tried to merge with the background, tried to hide Saga along with himself. Together, they backed away from the edge and under the cover of the trees.

From between the nearest branches, they saw the creature raise its muzzle in the air. Its mouth opened. Alfred wished he'd been the one wearing earmuffs, because the sound that rang out in the forest was terrifying.

It was the howl of a wolf, calling its pack. And the pack answered.

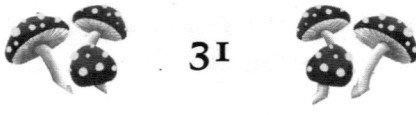

31

The Power of Names

Holding her by the wrist, Alfred pulled Saga along. Despite her earmuffs, he knew she'd heard the wolves too. Her pulse raced beneath his fingers. Her ragged breath sounded loud in the still, misty air. Even if he had known of a way to teach her his own invisibility trick, she wasn't calm enough for it to work.

The antlered wolf behind them howled again. It sounded closer. Howls answered from further away in the dark forest.

They hurried alongside the ravine. Alfred wanted to be close to the water. If the wolves caught up, he'd jump and deal with whatever was in the river.

Further downhill, the steep sides of the ravine widened. The distance to the river shrank. The noise of the rushing water increased, until it was so loud it drowned out the music of the eternal dance. It even muted the howling wolves.

Where the ground flattened, the river flowed fast, just an arm's length below ground level. Its song rang in Alfred's ears. But, like an opera in a foreign language, the meaning of the words escaped him. He knew he only had to stick his head under the surface to understand them. And he longed to listen to the story they were telling.

Alfred slowed. He shook his head and rubbed his ears, freeing himself from the grip of the music. They couldn't pause here. The wolf howls grew louder.

Ahead, Saga was waving him towards her. 'It's here,' she said. 'The tree trunk.'

Alfred trotted after her, but his heart sank when he saw the fallen trunk.

In the real world, the trunk bridge had only been three metres long, and he still hadn't made it across. Here, the river was wilder and wider. The distance was at least double, and slimy plants covered the decaying wood.

Underneath, long tendrils flowed just below the surface.

Beyond the river, the trees thinned. A path led over the plateau straight to the moonlit fortress.

He pushed one of the glittering earmuffs back behind Saga's ear.

'Take this.' He held the red sock containing the spy-figurine towards Saga. 'If I don't make it across...' He was still clutching the sock, as if his fingers didn't want to let go. This was the key to unlocking the secret of his heritage. His only bargaining leverage. But if Lillith attacked him, or perhaps threw him out of Faerie, Saga would need it. He would find another way to discover the truth. 'Whatever happens, keep going. Trade this for your shadow and a way out of Faerie, so you can stop everyone from touching those deadly plants.'

He could see she was about to object, when a clear voice behind them shouted, 'Intruders! That way.'

Alfred thrust the figurine into the opening at the side of Saga's shoulder bag, and then they were sprinting the last metres to the fallen tree.

Nimbly, Saga sprang up on the trunk. She was halfway across when a growl made Alfred turn round. Behind him, just a few metres away, slanting orange eyes glowed. An antlered wolf slunk nearer, its sharp fangs on full display. A foul-smelling greenish froth foamed at its mouth and dripped onto the ground.

'Keep going!' Alfred called.

He stepped up on the slippery, overgrown wood, and tried to walk as fast as possible without dislodging any of the creepers.

The wolf howled.

Glancing over his shoulder, he saw it standing on dry land, staring after him with those glowing eyes. In the water, the tendrils drifted towards the surface. In front of him, Saga had reached the other bank.

He almost made it across.

Perhaps it was the howling wolves catching up. Perhaps it was because he saw, a short way upriver ahead of him, the silhouette of a huge bear. Or perhaps it was the fact that a bat swooped down over the river and flew directly at him. Its mouth opened in a high-pitched shriek. A shriek that demanded him to follow.

Whatever the reason, Alfred wobbled.

A scatter of bark and moss fell into the water.

Even before the strands of hair reacted, he lost his balance. The only thing he had time to do before he hit the surface was to yell, 'Run!'

On his way to the depths, his only thoughts were for Saga. He hoped she would escape the wolves and the bear and the bat—if they'd been real and not just one of his nightmares.

As he pushed off from the riverbed, a shape swam towards him. It was the catfish from Granny's front room. Was this all a bad dream?

He pinched his arm, hoping to wake up in the narrow bed under the tapestry. But of course he wasn't sleeping.

With a swish of its tail, the catfish swam past him, singing, *'Breathe calmly.'*

It helped. He let the water flow in through his mouth and out of the dimples by his ears, while he listened to the underwater ballad.

The lyrics formed pictures in his mind. He saw the whole faerie world. A different faerie world. A beautiful place where plants grew wild, and all creatures lived peacefully together. A place where nature ruled.

From far away, another tale drifted his way. In it, the chorus mentioned Nereida. He even thought they sang his father's name.

That song tugged at his heart. It made him think of the little water sprite in his pocket. The music was begging him to come closer, begging him to stay in the depths and listen to the whole saga.

Saga! He couldn't stay. He had to help Saga.

Alfred had been so absorbed by the sung stories that he hadn't noticed the hair strands multiplying around him. With all his might, he frog-kicked and swam upwards.

As he broke the surface, a cool breeze kissed his fingertips. Then the strands tightened round his legs. In a heartbeat, the monstrous water sprite was upon him, clasping his shoulders with sharp nails, binding him with her hair.

She trussed his arms close to his sides, but he tried to worm his hand into the pocket with the water-sprite figurine. She belonged here in the river. If only he could reach her, she would give him strength.

'I told you to stay away,' Lillith said—or sang, if song could be this furious, with such a menacing undertone. 'How dare you come here?' She tugged at the hairband until his locks flowed freely.

With another push, Alfred got his fingers round the figurine in his pocket. When it nestled in his palm, a surge of relief went through him. This water sprite was on his side.

He didn't know if he could speak under water, but he tried saying, 'Let me go!' The words bubbled out of his mouth in a little tune. He couldn't believe what he was hearing. Neither, it seemed, could Lillith. Her big green eyes blinked, but she didn't let go.

Alfred tried again. 'Let me go!' he yelled. His words rose to a crescendo. A booming 'oh' resonated around him. He made as if to fill his lungs, though the water just gushed out by his ears, and sang, 'Lillith!'

At once, the strands that entangled him came undone. Lillith's hold on his arms slackened. Knowing her name had actually helped. Alfred sent a grateful thought to Amanita, while he pulled himself free and reached up to take a swim stroke. But he had forgotten that he was clutching the figurine.

Lillith's eyes grew even bigger when she saw it. Alfred had no time to react before she pounced. Gripping his wrist with one hand, she prised his fingers open with the other.

No matter how many times he yelled her name, she didn't let go until she'd torn the figurine from his hand. She held it up close to those big green eyes. A strange fanatical expression shone out of them.

The loss of the little water sprite was like a physical pain that coursed from Alfred's empty hand through the rest of his body. Even so, he took the opportunity while Lillith was distracted. With three breaststrokes he reached the riverbank.

Drenched, he crawled out of the soothing water, leaving behind his most cherished possession.

32

Antlers and Armour

Still on hands and knees, Alfred glanced around. He couldn't see Saga or any antlered wolves. While he'd been listening to the ballads and struggling with Lillith, the current had carried him downriver. The bear and the bat had been upstream from the tree trunk and were nowhere in sight.

He staggered out of reach of the hair strands, in among the nearest trees, although he wished he could jump back in the stream and wrestle with Lillith until she surrendered the figurine.

After catching his breath, he half ran upstream towards the tree trunk, sheltered by trees. Shouts from the other side of the river made him stop. From a thicket, he peered out between the twigs. There was a commotion by the tree-trunk bridge. From here, he could just see the tangle of antlers. Some antlers were much higher than others, and he heard voices from the group.

The open moonlit space and the path stretched between Alfred and the fortress. But as soon as he set off from the thicket, he would be visible from the tree trunk. First, he had to take a closer look at those wolves.

Still hidden by the trees, he sneaked nearer. Among the antlered wolves stood other creatures. A whole herd of them. They stood upright on two legs, but they had antlers too. Enormous antlers.

Below the antlers, their faces were humanoid. And so were their armour-plated torsos. They seemed to be deliberating before wanting to cross the river. Alfred wondered if they feared Lillith.

When some of them began traipsing across, he discovered another explanation. Like fauns from a fairy tale, their two hairy legs ended in hooves. They would have even more difficulty traversing the trunk than him. Taking this opportunity of getting away, he set off across the open space.

Immediately, he heard yells of, 'The intruder!' and 'Hurry!'

He kept running until the shouts became cries for help. A wolf howled in panic. Behind him, strands of Lillith's hair whipped through the air and curled itself round antlers. Three of the creatures were already in the water, trying to make their way back to their comrades.

He was almost by an archway to the fortress, when he heard a hissed, 'Psst!'

Saga detached herself from the shadows. Her earmuffs sparkled in the moonlight. Limping, she tugged him into a nook in the clammy wall.

'What's wrong with your foot?' he panted, as she freed one ear.

'It's nothing. Twisted my ankle. What happened?'

'Lillith let me go, the moment I said her name. But I lost...' Alfred swallowed. 'She took the water-sprite figurine. And just now she's stopping the guards from crossing.'

'Doesn't help. This place is full of guards. You won't believe, they have antlers and...' A glazed look came into Saga's eyes. She began swaying.

The eternal music was clear and beautiful here, but it didn't pull at Alfred like the music of the river. The same couldn't be said for Saga. As if he weren't even there, she took two dance steps towards the archway.

Alfred grabbed her arm with one hand and pulled the earmuff down with the other. Back in the shadows, she blinked a few times before her hands flew up to make sure her earmuffs were secure.

'I've been thinking...' she began. 'We can't get inside with so many guards. Do you honestly think Amanita will help us if she gets the spy figurine in return? Nod or shake your head.'

Amanita wanted the little woodcarving. One of them, at least. And now he had the perfect reason for not handing over the water sprite. Of course, with all the guards around, she would be able to seize the figurine without honouring the deal. But she could have taken it in the woods. It had seemed important that he gave it willingly. He nodded.

'Then you should try calling her,' Saga said. 'I will hide, with the spy figurine safely in here'—she thumped her shoulder bag—'until she appears. And if she doesn't come, if the guards capture you,' she began, voicing Alfred's own fears, 'you must ask them to take you to Amanita. Say you've promised to bring the queen something valuable. Make it clear that you don't have it on your person but have hidden it and will only reveal where it is to her. Or something like that. Just don't tell a direct lie.'

Alfred nodded again. There wasn't anything more to say. After a deep inhale, he walked out in front of the archway. He stood, visible in the moonlight, and called, 'Amanita,' once. It didn't take more than a few seconds before he heard hoofbeats. Dozens of guards galloped out of the fortress and surrounded him.

He tried not to shrink back from them. It was hard, with so many pairs of eyes staring down at him. Eyes that were cloudy and whitish, like those of dead fish. He didn't want to look at their antlers or hooves either, so he focused his gaze on the wide shoulders and the armour that covered their torsos. The metal was matt and dented and scratched. Battle-tested.

'Messenger! Tell the queen's consort we have caught the intruder,' the guard with the largest antlers said.

After what felt like an eternity, where no one spoke, all the guards stood to attention. In salute, they raised their right arms and flicked their antlers with their fingers, so a low hum resonated from the branched horns.

'Your excellency, we have captured the intruder,' the head guard said. His salute made all sixteen points on his antlers vibrate.

A faerie so tall he would tower over professional basketball players strode between them. Above high cheekbones, his dark eyes were as bottomless as Amanita's. By his side hung a sword with green gemstones on the hilt. The armour that covered his chest and arms gleamed. Six orange-speckled butterfly faeries that reminded Alfred of the Duke of Burgundy sat on his shoulders. At first glance, they looked like the epaulette stars on a high-ranking officer, but each of them had a tiny cloth in their hands. They were busy moving their arms in circles, polishing the armour.

Alfred mustered his courage, looked up at the queen's consort, and said, 'Take me to Amanita. She'll want to see me. I've made a deal with her.'

'Amanita?' the queen's consort repeated, glaring at Alfred.

Should he ask to be taken to the queen? Amanita had said the queen wanted the woodcarving. But she'd meant the water sprite, not the fork-tongued spy that the queen surely had innumerable copies of. And it was one thing to cheat a normal faerie in a deal... Could he trick the faerie queen everyone feared?

'Or the queen! I have something she wants,' he said in his panic.

The consort didn't deign to answer. After giving a minute shake of his head, he turned away and left, to the sound of humming antlers.

The head guard ordered, 'Take him to the dungeons.'

Two guards, gripping his arms, led him in through the archway, while he yelled, 'Amanita!'

Other guards marched in front and behind him, leaving him no escape.

From outside the walls, he heard a clamour.

Saga screamed.

'Mr Tumbleweed!' she shouted. 'Mr Tumbleweed, help!'

As the guards ushered him across a courtyard, Alfred called for Amanita again.

'Help us stop the tunnel,' Saga called behind him.

In a corner, a gathering of imposing faeries glanced their way, before they continued their conversation. A girl with long black hair looked on from an open window above. She could've been human if not for her skin, which glittered in a kaleidoscope of darkening colours.

Alfred's guards ducked to get their antlers through a low door in the thick fortress wall. Here, they paused until the guards that were escorting Saga caught up. Then they herded both of them down steep stairs.

Saga kept shouting, the sound loud in the narrow space, until the leader called for someone to shut her up.

An eclipse of moths fluttered towards them.

Saga cried, 'Mr Tum—' Like a rag doll, she slumped into the arms of the nearest guard.

Alfred tried to look away from the moths. He tried to squeeze his eyes shut. But he could do neither. Although the moths didn't touch him, it was as if their grey-brown wings beat at his eyelashes, forcing his eyelids to part. Transfixed, he watched them fly towards his face in ever smaller spirals. They whirled round and round until it seemed like they were inside his head. Then everything grew dark, and he blacked out.

33

A Cage in a Cave

Freezing cold, Alfred came to his senses. His cheek pressed into the uneven rock of a stone floor. His clothes were still damp. Saga lay facing him, so close he could feel her breath. Her glasses hung lopsided across her forehead.

On the wall beyond their feet, a dim light from a flame glowed silver. It cast shadow stripes of prison bars over them. They were inside a cage in a cave—imprisoned in the faerie dungeons.

Between them, by their hips, lay Saga's bag. Its shoulder strap had slid down her arm. The clasps were closed. The hourglass, still attached to Saga's belt loop, had smashed and the sand had leaked out amid splintered wood and glass shards.

Voices murmured behind him.

Cautiously, Alfred turned over onto his other side. Beyond the prison bars that surrounded them, an opening in the rock wall led to another cave. In there, two guards sat at a table, in much brighter silvery light. They were playing a game with pebbles they threw up in the air.

He rolled back to face Saga. To avoid attracting the guards' attention, he blew on her face. She didn't stir.

Without trying to sit up, he scooted down until he could stick his hand into the shoulder bag. He rummaged inside. Guessing what he was touching was like playing a child's sensory game. The flashlight, a water bottle, the notebook, several pens, a long heavy nail, a zipper, extra batteries, hairbands, a candle, matches, a pack of tissues, a bundle of yarn and something soft, probably her scarf. Nothing felt like the fork-tongued figurine.

The gap at the side of the bag was large enough for his arm. Could the woodcarving have fallen out while Saga was running? Or perhaps the guards had searched her bag and taken it, leaving everything else.

He had almost given up, when he noticed a lump under the canvas. It was just the right size to be the spy. He slid his other hand underneath the bag. Nothing. But then he felt the lump through the fabric. Alfred almost laughed out loud. A zipper! There was a zippered compartment in the bag.

Noiselessly, he loosened one clasp, got both hands inside and opened the zipper. Wiggling them into the red sock, his fingers touched the forked tongue. He shuddered, then closed the zipper again. They still had the spy figurine. They still had bargaining power.

He sat up and shook Saga gently. When she opened her eyes, he put a finger to his lips. She fumbled for her glasses. While she pushed herself up, her eyes roamed.

'The spy is still in your bag. I checked,' he whispered.

Saga pointed at the smashed hourglass, whispering, 'How long?'

Alfred shrugged.

'Have you tried sneaking out between those trees?'

He shook his head. Now that he was sitting up, he saw that the prison bars were slender tree trunks. On the side where their heads had been while they'd been lying down, the trunks were so far apart they could slip out between them.

Before getting up, though, his gaze slid upwards. Above, pale grey leaves grew on branches that hung down like those of weeping willows. He wondered if there was an opening to the outside in the cave ceiling. Perhaps then they could climb the odd colourless trees to escape. To see better, he leant back. As he did, the hanging fronds moved as one, following him, like metallic threads drawn towards a magnet.

'Awake, are you?' One of the guards stood in the arch between the caves. His antlers cast shadows like twigs that were crawling towards them. He turned back to the other guard, saying, 'You lost the game. Find the queen's consort.'

'Wait!' Alfred called.

Both guards stepped into their cave.

'Can you please find Amanita? I've made a deal with her.'

Frowning, the guards watched him.

The second guard said, 'There is no one of that name here.'

Alfred sank back. Of course. He hadn't given Amanita his real name, why would she have given him hers? But he wasn't giving up.

'She's tall and has long whitish hair,' he began.

'Oh, her,' the first guard said.

'You know her?'

'Yeah, her and all the other high faeries that fit your description.' He smirked.

'My tree-sprite friend would want to know I'm here,' Saga said, sounding almost convinced.

The second guard just shook his head, giving his antlers a swirl. 'As if a lowly stick insect dared entered the fortress.'

Both guards guffawed.

Alfred's mind raced. Earlier, when he'd asked to be taken to the queen, he'd been panicking. He hadn't thought through the consequences of trying to trick her and Amanita. Now he did.

If the queen discovered his deception, she would make them dance the eternal dance. Or rather, she would make Saga dance the eternal dance. For him, with his faerie blood, she might have a much worse punishment in store. Perhaps she'd capture his essence in a wood-carved sculpture.

Without wanting to, he imagined being imprisoned inside a piece of wood, standing in the dripstone cavern next to Holly Blue.

Still, what choice did they have?

'Take us to the faerie queen,' Alfred finally said. 'She'll be angry at you if she doesn't get what I have brought for her.'

The guards stopped smirking.

'The queen is away,' the first one said.

'Luckily for us, her consort has much more interesting games to play with humans. It's so boring just to watch you dance.'

Saga whimpered, a hand over her mouth to mute the sound.

Lillith had said Alfred was reckless, as reckless as Nereida. She'd told him to stay away. She'd warned him. Why hadn't he listened?

In the other cave, the guards were guffawing again.

'I hope he's planning a chase,' one of them said.

The second guard set off to find the queen's consort, his hooves clacking on the stone steps. He called over his shoulder, 'The beasts are mighty hungry... Did you hear them howl?'

Saga paled. 'What about my family?' she whispered. 'They'll never know what happened to us.' She sobbed.

Alfred closed his eyes. A lump was growing in his throat. He thought of a double funeral with empty coffins, seven years from now, before he forced his thoughts away.

He'd believed being imprisoned in the spirit cavern was the worst that could happen. Being chased and eaten by a pack of antlered wolves as entertainment for the guards seemed an infinitely worse fate.

34

Somebody Returns

Alfred cradled his head in his hands and tried to stop his brain from running amok. Like strobe lights, images flashed in his mind: the froth around sharp canine teeth, glowing orange eyes, Dad's sad eyes, Lillith's furious expression, moss landing in the river.

If only they could make it to the river. But, unless they got a head start, that was impossible.

It took a while before he realized Saga was nudging him. She pointed to the next cave. The first guard sat at the table, sorting the pebbles.

'We won't get another chance,' she whispered. 'I'm going to sneak out and hide next to the archway. Then you call him in here, and I'll hit him on the head with this.' She lifted her flashlight.

It wasn't much of a plan, but it was better than doing nothing. Alfred didn't want to think about how many guards they would have to pass outside the cave before they were free.

Saga got to her feet. But when she tried to put weight on the foot she had twisted, her leg collapsed, and she gasped in pain. They both looked down at her swollen ankle. It seemed ironic that suddenly she was the one who couldn't walk.

'Give me the flashlight,' he whispered and took it from her hands.

When he moved towards one of the prison bars, a low whoosh went through the air right above his head. The hanging fronds followed his movement. Out of the corner of his eye, he saw how those furthest away seemed to grow longer.

Without touching the slender trees, he prepared to step sideways through a gap. But the instant his foot crossed the invisible line between the trunks, tiny shoots grew from them, at a speed that made them look like blurred lines. Alfred tried to pull his leg back, but the shoots ensnared it. In mere moments, they'd grown together in a strong weave. Above him, the hanging fronds stretched. Leaves tangled themselves into his hair, and the willowy branches twisted their way round his neck.

'Don't move,' Saga said.

Alfred stood stock still. The plants stopped growing.

'Hey,' the guard called, getting up.

They watched as something hit him behind the antlers. He fell forward, landing with a thump and a crack. Into view hopped a giant stick insect.

Mr Tumbleweed stopped outside their living prison.

'I knew you hadn't deserted me!'

'If a body doesn't want another body who has been protecting them all their life to go away, then that body shouldn't banish this one body that is only doing their job,' he said in his groaning-floorboard voice.

'I can understand you!' For a brief moment, Saga looked happy, then she appeared to remember their situation. 'I'm sorry, I didn't mean to send you away.'

Alfred was still trying to figure out what Mr Tumbleweed had said. It seemed they had been right. He had been protecting Saga against other faeries.

'The little people took my shadow. It would never have happened with you by my side.'

'If a body banishes this one body who was forced to protect them, but still didn't always mind their job, then that body must expect that other bodies who have no obligations towards a human body will take advantage of the situation.'

'Why didn't you just tell Saga you were protecting her?' Alfred asked.

'Just because a body can speak doesn't mean they want to say anything. And even if they want to say something, it doesn't mean they can, if some other body doesn't want them to be able to speak in a manner that can be understood by a human body.'

'So someone forced you to protect Saga from faeries, but prevented you from speaking to her?'

The tree sprite opened his gash mouth to speak, but Alfred stopped him, saying, 'No need to answer. We don't have that much time. The other guard can return at any moment with the queen's consort, who is probably bringing half a garrison.'

'And if the body this one body protects likes a rude abomination—' Mr Tumbleweed muttered under his breath until Saga stopped him with a new question.

'Can you help us get out of here?'

Alfred prepared for another long answer filled with bodies. But Mr Tumbleweed simply said, 'No.'

'Too many guards, is that it?' Saga asked. 'Can you get hold of Amanita? Al... Nemo has made a deal with her. We think she can help us. I know there is no one of that name here, but she's the faerie we saw—you saw her too—up by the sinkhole the other day.'

Mr Tumbleweed's head twirled from side to side as he began to shake. Getting down on all four twiggy limbs, he steadied himself.

His gravelly voice shook when he spoke again. 'This one body can find the faerie who called herself Amanita if that is truly what the body this one body was bound to protect for so long desires.'

'Thank you, Mr Tumbleweed. I know that isn't your name and that you won't want to tell me your real name here.'

'I don't think we have much time before the guard returns. Can you hurry?' Alfred said. 'Please?'

The tree sprite turned away and took a giant hop.

'Hey! Can you help me get free of these branches first?' Alfred's foot was still stuck, and at the slightest turn of his head the entangled hanging fronds tore at his hair.

'No. This one body doesn't have time, because this one body has to find another body, before the bodyguards are coming, and this one body...' The creaking voice grew fainter until they couldn't hear it at all.

Alfred tried to shift his weight into a less uncomfortable position. He leant into the branches that had tangled themselves round his neck until they supported him. At least it was his short leg that had been caught by the tree shoots.

'I'm so happy he came back,' Saga said. 'I knew he would.'

Alfred didn't remind her how she'd doubted Mr Tumbleweed would ever return. Even he couldn't stop a tiny bud of hope from sprouting.

If only Mr Tumbleweed hurried to find Amanita. As part of the deal, she'd promised to protect them. She was a high faerie, and she could defend them against the guards. Could she keep them safe from the queen's consort too?

'I really hope Mr Tumbleweed will come home with me,' Saga said. 'I'm just not me without him, you know?'

A loud thump from the next cave prevented Alfred from answering. The light that shone through the archway was blocked by a gigantic shape. The shape of a giant bear.

35

Chased

The bear shape sniffed.

Saga gripped Alfred's arm.

'It's him alright,' a deep bass voice rumbled. 'I said we could trust the rooks. It's really hurtful when you don't listen to me.'

'I don't trust birds,' another voice hissed, with quick clipped words.

'I can see why they would be untrustworthy with their black wings and scary ways. They don't at all remind me of anyone else around here,' the first voice said.

'Just focus on the task, Bjørn.'

The looming shape lumbered into the light from the silver torch. As his enormous feet shuffled nearer, he scratched his rotund belly through an opening between two buttons on his hairy coat. He wasn't a bear, although he almost looked like one. He most definitely wasn't human either. Especially, his nose looked out of place. It was a black-tipped snout with gaping, receptive nostrils.

He sniffed again. 'Oh, dear! The stench of fear in here. It makes me quite peckish.'

'Hurry up.'

'The guard out there isn't waking up anytime soon. I gave him a soft punch, just to make sure he got a full night's sleep.'

'I'm not talking about him,' the clipped voice hissed. 'Ten guards on level five are stomping their way down here.'

Alfred couldn't hear anything.

'Who are you?' Saga asked.

'There's absolutely no reason to be afraid.' Bjørn grinned, in what was probably meant to be a friendly way. Crow's feet fanned out in his weather-beaten brown face, but fangs gleamed in his dark beard.

He seized two of the living cage's slender trunks, his claw-like fingernails scraping deep into the bark, making the trees weep sap. Then he plucked them from the rock, as if he were pulling weeds out of soft soil.

A girl stepped under Bjørn's arm, into the cage. Her skin was midnight dark. She wore black jeans, long black boots and a black leather jacket. Her cropped black hair made little peaks on top of her head. Everything from her button nose to her hands with their black varnished nails was tiny, except her ears. Her ears were large and strange and studded with rows of sparkling gemstones.

'Help me with his foot,' she said, and cut into one of the fronds round Alfred's neck with a pair of sharp scissors that resembled the ones Granny used for snipping off threads. As one, the tips of all the other hanging branches let go of him and slithered upwards. Meanwhile Bjørn scratched across the shoots that twirled round Alfred's leg, with his hairy clawed feet.

'Come on, Alfred,' the girl said, looking up at him.

'You know my name? Who are you?'

The girl just raised an eyebrow. 'And you, human—'

'Saga,' Saga said, and limped out of the cage after him.

'You can call me Batty.' She glared at them, as if daring any of them to make a joke. 'Help me with the human, Bjørn.'

In the next cave, the guard slumped on the ground, face down. A few of his antler tips had broken off and lay scattered among the pebbles he'd been sorting.

Bjørn's close-set brown eyes twinkled in the bright light. Alfred noticed the embroidery on his coat. Colourful flowers, with bees flying between them, bloomed all over the back and front. It seemed to be a work in progress because one sleeve was bare, and a silken thread hung from a half-finished rose on the shoulder.

Bjørn caught him staring. 'Do you like it? I'm so delighted with how it's turning out. Except that one.' He pointed at a bee on the left elbow. Something was wrong with the angle of its wings. 'It was the first one I made, but you can't really see the mistake unless you know it's there. I just wish I'd had time to finish before—'

'Less talk, Bjørn,' Batty interrupted. 'Let's go.'

'I can't leave without Mr Tumbleweed.'

'Or your shadow,' Alfred added.

'Shadows are overrated,' Batty said. 'You don't need them at night.'

'But she'll be going outside in sunshine.'

'We don't have time for this.' Batty pushed Saga towards Bjørn. 'Be quiet.'

'Don't you be scared now, darling. I've got you,' Bjørn said and swung Saga up on his wide shoulder. 'What about you, honey? Can I give you a lift too? It's honestly no bother.'

It took a moment before Alfred realized Bjørn was talking to him and not to Batty. At the same time, he understood that they were being taken away. 'Wait! Where're you taking us? We have to wait for Amanita.'

'We're not waiting for anyone,' Batty hissed.

'Then I'm staying.' Alfred tried to put force into his voice without raising it. 'Amanita can protect us. I've made a deal with her and she knows the queen.'

At the last word, Bjørn's eyes widened, showing a white ring round their brown centre. 'Please don't mention Her,' he whispered. 'We're not on Her side.'

'Bjørn, that's enough.' Batty stepped right in front of Alfred and glared up at him. 'You're coming with us. And if you don't stop shouting, I'll gag you.'

Alfred was about to say that he wasn't shouting, that if he'd spoken any quieter, he would've been whispering, and that he wanted to know more about them before he'd agree to come with them. But he didn't get an opportunity to reply.

A siren went off somewhere. A spy siren. Batty covered her ears with both hands. All the silvery torches extinguished. They were surrounded by absolute darkness.

Moments later, the siren stopped. Wolves howled. The clopping of hooves echoed on the stone steps, growing louder.

Alfred felt Bjørn throw him up onto his hairy shoulder and grab hold of his knees. The giant creature began running, jostling the children from side to side.

Saga whimpered something about Mr Tumbleweed.

Alfred reached behind Bjørn's neck and found one of her hands. Dangling, heads down on that hairy back, they held on to each other. Bjørn's thumping footfalls drowned out the sound of hoofbeats but not the howling of the antlered wolves.

'I hope Marjorie has finished digging,' Bjørn panted.

There was no answer from Batty.

Perhaps she had sprinted ahead. Alfred couldn't hear the clacking of her high-heeled boots. She seemed to be in charge and deciding what to do and how much to tell them. Bjørn had said they weren't on the queen's side. What other sides were there? The queen's consort's side? Was this all part of an elaborate plan that would end with them being eaten by the wolves?

When the silvery torches began gleaming again, Alfred raised his head. Behind them, he saw a blur of antlers. The guards were springing after them, gaining on them, with the speed of four-legged stags.

36

Across the Desolation

Suddenly, Bjørn stopped. Alfred was thrown upwards, before his stomach landed hard on Bjørn's shoulder again.

'Down here,' a small voice peeped.

'Blooming bloomers,' Bjørn said. 'Couldn't you've warned me, Batty?'

'Uh, I hope we've made it big enough.' The peeping voice sounded anxious.

'No need to fret, Marjorie. You've done a wonderful job.'

'Thank you, dear. Go ahead. I'll see if we can close before they catch up.'

Bjørn climbed down into a hole. 'Ah,' he said, 'A bit of a squeeze.'

'I can walk.' Alfred slid down until he was standing in front of Bjørn.

The rough walls of a newly dug tunnel led away from the hole. The only light came from the main tunnel behind them. A few loose stones tumbled after them through the entrance and then a small rockfall half-closed the opening, taking most of the light.

Bjørn shifted Saga's body so that he was cradling her in

his arms and she wouldn't bump against the tunnel ceiling. Behind the giant, Alfred caught a glimpse of small creatures digging and scraping inside a cascade of dust.

'You'd better be able to run,' Batty said right next to him. Where had she come from? She thrust a silver-glowing torch into his hand. 'And do it now. After me.' Her heels clacked a couple of times before she was gone.

Limping slightly, Alfred ran. The reach of the torch only illuminated the next metre, but that was all he needed to see where to place his feet. He feared twisting his right ankle on its raised heel. His legs were stiff after lying on that cold stone floor.

When he came out into an old tunnel, Alfred stopped to catch his breath. But before Bjørn and Saga caught up, Batty snarled, 'Come on!'

This tunnel continued downwards, in an almost straight line. He could feel the strain on the front of his shins and thighs. But at least the ground was more even, so he worried less about where he placed his feet. He tried to focus on his breathing and avoid thinking about what might happen next.

A light appeared at the end of the tunnel. Seeing it gave him a burst of energy. Just before he reached the opening, a bird or a bat flew out ahead of him.

Outside, duo moonlight shone. Batty stood, leaning against a lonely tree. Her head was tilted back, her eyes roaming somewhere far above.

Alfred gulped air, his hands on his thighs. Bjørn came out of the tunnel and set Saga down. She looked dazed.

After he'd caught his breath, Alfred turned to see what Batty was studying. A high rock face loomed behind them.

'We're on the opposite side of the forest,' Saga said. 'That's the scenic lookout point.' She turned round. 'Remember, we saw the other prehistoric volcano from up there.' She pointed at the distant cone shape they'd seen from the top of the cliff. Like a gigantic molehill, it grew from the barren plain that stretched out beyond the lonely tree. A bonfire still glowed near the peak.

'That's where we're going,' Batty said. 'To the abandoned faerie fort.'

'But we need to find Amanita,' Alfred muttered.

Ignoring him, Bjørn asked, 'The long way, right?'

Before Batty could answer, Alfred heard a howl from the forest behind them. Somewhere out of sight, but nearby, other wolves answered.

'The beasts won't want to cross the desolation. Take the direct route,' Batty said. 'Sorry, old friend.' She sounded almost kind.

Bjørn slung Saga up on his shoulder again. At a jog, Alfred followed them through tall grass, past the lonely tree, out onto the plain. Wherever they were going had to be better than an encounter with the antlered wolves.

He'd expected to breathe easier in the open landscape. Instead, nausea hit him with a suddenness that made him want to curl up on the ground or crawl back into the tunnel. An acrid scent filled his nostrils. The air stank of burnt rubber. Every breath rasped in his throat.

'Sorry, darling.' Bjørn slowed to a walk. He huffed and lowered Saga to the ground. 'Can't carry you across here. My mojo's going.'

Batty's head swirled from side to side. She cupped her hands behind her ears as if trying to hear something far away. 'Hoofbeats,' she said. 'Hurry!'

Alfred couldn't hear anything but the occasional howl. Not even the slightest whisper of grass or leaves fluttering. There was no grass, he realized. Black rubble, like lava stones, covered the entire plain, as if the ancient volcanoes had recently spouted their molten rock over the landscape.

'Stay low,' Batty barked.

Hunched, they followed her, seeking cover behind some of the bigger black rocks. Bjørn seemed to be struggling even more than Alfred.

'What happened here? What is this place?' Saga asked. Holding on to Bjørn's embroidered sleeve, she hobbled along, wincing in pain every time she put weight on her foot.

'I've forgotten what you call it,' Bjørn huffed. 'One of those places where many humans live.'

'A housing estate?'

'That's not it.'

'They call it a city,' Batty hissed. 'And everywhere you humans build cities, our land is destroyed and becomes yet another expanse of desolation.'

The shock made Alfred stop. 'Every city does this to the faerie realm?' he asked, thinking back to the sprawling metropolitan areas where he'd lived.

'That's horrible!' Saga said. 'Would the tunnel do that to the Faerie Hill?'

'Oh, darling.' Bjørn patted her shoulder. 'That and worse. I followed your scent to the spirit prison cavern—'

'Morning sun and mermaids,' Batty swore. 'They're coming!'

At first, three antlered guards appeared, then an entire army trooped out of the tunnel mouth.

'Wouldn't it be safer to leave Faerie?' Alfred asked.

'For you, yes,' Batty said. 'But that's not part of our plan.'

The guards stopped by the lonely tree. Perhaps they wouldn't pursue them across the desolation. Or couldn't.

'Watch out,' Saga called.

Dozens of arrows flew towards them. One of them grazed Bjørn's shoulder, exactly where Saga had been hanging a little while ago, tearing the threads of an embroidered bee.

'I'll get help,' Batty said. She pirouetted on the spot, her garments fleetingly fluid around her. Then she vaporized in an inky swirl. Out of the dispersing vapour, a small black bat sped towards the cliff.

Another cluster of arrows swooshed around them, landing with a machine-gun rattle on the stones. Bjørn lumbered ahead, as they zigzagged between the larger rocks, heading for the volcano in the distance. Alfred's lungs felt like they were about to explode.

When he next glanced back, small black shapes swarmed out of gaps in the pale cliff face. They surrounded the antlered guards in a dark cloud. Few arrows were let loose from inside the cloud, and none of them came near their targets. Neither antlered wolves nor guards ventured out onto the desolation.

'Are we outside their range? Can we stop for a moment?' Saga asked. 'I want to bind my scarf round my ankle.'

'I'll help you.' Bjørn knelt and pulled off Saga's hiking boot, mumbling soothing words, as she winced.

While he was tying her bandage in place, with surprising dexterity for someone with such big hands, Alfred studied him. The bear-like creature didn't seem to wish them harm. He and Batty hadn't been part of the queen's consort's wolf-chase scheme. But they were definitely hiding something.

'Batty mentioned a plan. Tell us what it is,' Alfred said.

'I'm sorry.' Bjørn looked at them with his kind eyes. 'It's really nothing personal, and I wouldn't try to escape if I were you—Batty does have rather a lot of friends with sharp teeth—but,' he sighed, 'we have kidnapped you and plan to demand a ransom.'

37

The Bear and the Bat

'What ransom?' Saga asked. 'If it's money you're after, then good luck. Dad's been trying to get a loan for a new tractor for ages.'

'Why would we want human money?' Bjørn shook his head, while tying the last knot on Saga's impromptu bandage. 'What we want is an end to the drilling of holes in our hill.'

'That's what we want too!'

'How could kidnapping us stop the tunnel project?' Alfred asked.

'Batty will explain everything when we see her at the old faerie fort. Now let's go.'

'It's nothing personal, Bjørn, but we're not going anywhere, and you can't carry us across this desolation.' Saga patted the stony ground. 'Come and sit next to me, Alfred.'

'Now listen here...' Bjørn looked back towards the cliff, with a worried frown. Alfred followed his gaze. Under the cloud of bats, the guards retreated into the tunnel. 'You don't want to upset Batty. She can be rather...'

A black shape shot towards them at incredible speed. Like a gathering storm cloud, it appeared to suck in dark particles. While descending, this darkness solidified into the spiky-haired bat girl. She stamped a high-heeled boot down mid-twirl. 'What can I be? And why are you not on your way to the abandoned fort?'

'It's... I... They...' Bjørn spluttered.

'He told us your plan,' Alfred said.

Saga crossed her arms. 'And we're not going anywhere until you tell us everything.' She was back to her own plucky self. Probably because Mr Tumbleweed had answered her call. Perhaps it also helped that she'd been carried most of the way through the underground and seemed to be less affected by the horrible air quality in the desolation.

Batty also crossed her arms. 'Alfred's father is in charge of that destructive project. He can put an end to it, if the life of his son is at risk.'

'That's not how these things work. My dad might be the boss, but that doesn't mean he can just decide to cancel the project. In the human world, politicians and government departments and committees decide.'

'Your grandmother always talks about him as if he can do anything,' Bjørn said.

'Yes, but she's his mother. Wait a minute... Can you hear everything that's going on in the cottage?' Alfred asked, remembering how the ears of the bat carving often seemed to twitch.

'Batty can. I mainly notice the mouth-watering aromas.'

'We're against the tunnel project too,' Saga said. 'And so is your queen. She has sent these weird creepers out into the real world. They've covered the whole building site. But they're poisonous.'

'Say what you will, Bjørn, at least the queen has always done everything in her power to protect our realm.'

'Batty! Please don't talk about Her, darlings.'

'In any case, there's no way you can trade us for the tunnel project,' Alfred said.

'We'll see about that. Now get moving or I'll bite you.' Batty bared her teeth.

'Bite me if you have to,' Saga said. 'I know you can't harm Alfred.'

'What did you tell them?' Batty hissed.

'I... no-nothing,' Bjørn stammered. Even kneeling, he was towering over Batty's large ears.

Alfred looked at Saga in surprise.

Saga smiled. 'I don't quite know how, but they must be bound to protect you, and not just your granny's cottage,' she said. 'Not exactly like Mr Tumbleweed... but somehow...'

Alfred thought about the woodcarvings and his nightmares. The bear, the bat, the eagle and perhaps the mole and the catfish had all appeared in his bad dreams. But had they been the villains? Or had they actually been trying to save him from the horrendous fork-tongued spy?

Bjørn had been nothing but kind to them. A catfish had told him to breathe calmly when he fell in the river, and Marjorie, who must be the mole, had dug a tunnel to help them escape the dungeons. His feeling that he recognized the eagle who'd flown straight at him during his first meeting with Amanita must've been correct. At the time, he'd thought it was attacking him, but it had also prevented him from going with the faerie. And then there was Batty. She was tough and hard to read, but she had saved them from captivity and hindered the arrow attack.

'So how does the protection work?' he asked.

'If we knew and could free ourselves, do you think we'd be here?' Batty said.

'I don't mind,' Bjørn added in his deep rumble. 'But we're just shapeshifters. The workings of high faeries are beyond us.'

'But are you... Are the carvings in Granny's cottage... Are they like the spirit prisons?' Alfred asked.

'Of course not.' Batty shook her head so the large ears fluttered. 'We're here, aren't we?'

'As I said, I followed your scent. I know you passed through the spirit prison cavern. If the humans drill anywhere near, if that place is destroyed, all those souls...' Bjørn choked. 'My dear Teddy, my old friends Ursu and Arth, Batty's sister, Marjorie's daughter Mollie...' A big tear rolled down into his beard. 'They would all be lost for ever. At least now there's hope.'

Saga leant forward to pat his arm.

'What about this one?' Alfred opened the zippered compartment in Saga's shoulder bag and extracted the fork-tongued figurine from the red sock.

'Put that away at once,' Batty hissed.

'What did you have to do that for?' Bjørn covered the spy with his enormous hand.

'You shouldn't *ever* take that out of the cottage.' For the first time since Alfred had met her, Batty looked frightened. Her head whirred round, looking in all directions, while he stuffed the figurine into his pocket.

'Why?' Alfred asked. 'It's one of Her spies.' It seemed that every time he uncovered something, he just found new unanswerable questions. But one faerie had promised him answers. 'I'm giving it away.'

'You can't do that!' Batty said.

'He thinks he cheated this faerie and the queen, because he believes they really wanted another figurine.' Saga closed her bag.

'They definitely want that one.' Batty pointed at his pocket. 'And nothing good ever comes of cheating a high faerie.'

'I've promised it in exchange for help to stop the tunnel, protection and information about my parents.' Choosing his words carefully, so as not to lie about it being part of the deal, he added, 'And we need Saga's shadow.'

'But we're protecting you. And we can tell you all about your parents,' Bjørn said.

'Who took your shadow?' Batty asked.

Saga didn't answer. She was staring at her shoulder bag, fingering her nature group badge, deep in thought.

'Little Mother and Little Father,' Alfred said.

'Of course.' Batty sighed, sounding tired. 'We need to get moving. The guards will be alerting the queen's consort or some other high faerie. And unlike the guards and their beasts, the high faeries have no problem crossing the desolation.'

'I'm not going anywhere before you tell me about my parents.'

Bjørn opened his mouth to speak, but Batty said, 'Then I think we're at an impasse, because we're not letting you go, and we're not telling you anything—not a word, Bjørn—before your father has promised there will be no drilling into our hill.'

'I have an idea,' Saga said. 'I think I know how we can stop the tunnel project.'

38

A Forced Promise

Saga spoke quickly, explaining her plan.

'You said you followed our scent to the cave with the spirit prisons, Bjørn. Did you also pass through the other cavern? The one with all the beautiful dripstones.'

Bjørn nodded.

'It must be close to the tunnel building site. Remember, we found that yellow measuring thingy—'

'The theodolite,' Alfred said. While he listened, he was scanning the cliff above the dark cloud of bats. A pack of the antlered wolves stood on the edge by the scenic viewpoint. As he watched, the beasts split up and ran along the clifftop, howling messages to each other and the guards.

Batty stood, ears quivering, drumming her black-lacquered nails against each other. 'Get to the point. The beasts will soon cover the entire perimeter of the forest.'

'Yes. That cavern is a natural wonder, and I think even the mayor will realize it's worth preserving if he sees it. But can you get into the cavern from our realm?' Saga asked. 'Without falling through a sinkhole, I mean.'

'We'll need to ask Marjorie,' Bjørn said.

'Will that really be enough for the humans? It's nothing special.' Batty frowned. 'What do you think, Alfred?'

Alfred glanced from Saga to Batty. The plan was clever, but he shared Batty's concern. 'Yeah, I think seeing the dripstone cave will convince them,' he said, trying to keep doubt out of his voice. 'But all the decisions at Dad's work always take ages—weeks or months. Do we have time?'

'We just need the mayor to agree,' Saga replied. 'He's like a human bulldozer.'

'That seems fair, Batty,' Bjørn said. 'If the pixies haven't handed over the shadow yet, Evie can—'

'So we're supposed to just let you go, based on this feeble scheme?' Batty interrupted. 'Nice try! In exchange, you, Alfred, must promise to leave that thing'—Batty pointed at his pocket again—'the figurine you showed us that has a serpent's tongue. You must promise to leave it in the window above the door of your grandmother's cottage, and that you won't ever give it or trade it away to anyone.'

'Couldn't we tell him a little bit about his parents first?' asked Bjørn.

'No!'

Alfred considered his options. If he made this promise, and Saga's plan didn't work, Batty and Bjørn wouldn't tell him anything. Neither would Amanita. He'd be worse off than when he'd arrived at Granny's cottage. But if it did work, they might be able to save the Faerie Hill, save Faerie itself, and he'd finally know the truth about his parents.

'It's going to work,' Saga said, taking his hand and squeezing it.

Alfred got to his feet. 'It's a deal. I promise. But tell me why you want that spy inside the cottage.'

'No time. There are high faeries in the tunnels,' Batty said. 'Now, get moving. Take them around the hill, Bjørn. I'll get you cover.'

Before Saga and Bjørn had even stood up, Batty was a bat and flying towards the limestone cliff. When she arrived there, the cloud of bats changed shape and flew nearer. It grew and stretched until it hid the forest from view. Under its cover, Saga, Bjørn and Alfred plodded their way along the hill.

Above them the antlered wolves howled, and somewhere behind guards shouted orders, but they remained hidden by the bats.

When they had put some distance between themselves and the mouth of the tunnel, they made their way back towards the forest. They knew they'd reached the boundary of the city, where plants shot out of the black rubble. Soon, greenery covered the ground, and they left the desolation behind.

Alfred filled his lungs with the slightly mouldy air.

'I'm going to take on my other shape. And carry you,' Bjørn wheezed. 'I'll be much faster. And able to smell the wolves. No need to be scared. I'm not hungry.'

The transformation seemed to start from his shaggy coat. Its hairy threads contracted until they were very clearly fur. This fur spread down his legs and arms and up his neck, merging with his beard, moulding itself to his features, as they changed and he expanded.

In his human-like form, Bjørn was huge. The bear that appeared in his place was even bigger. On all fours, its back was level with the top of Alfred's head. After it lay down on its stomach, it blinked at them with Bjørn's kind eyes. A few dried blossoms were stuck in the soft, brown fur. Alfred couldn't spot any bees.

'Thanks, Bjørn.' Saga climbed up on the bear's wide shoulders.

Alfred clambered up behind her and held on to her waist. While Bjørn got to his paws, she leant forward, wrapping her arms round his thick neck. And then they were off.

Bjørn galloped so fast tears ran from Alfred's eyes. Above them, the bats swarmed. As they sped alongside the cliff face, it grew steadily smaller until it wasn't higher than a garden wall. Without slowing, Bjørn leapt up on top of the limestone cliff and entered the forest.

The colony of bats reacted to the sudden move with a slight delay.

Immediately, howls of alarm rang out from several directions.

Bjørn charged uphill through the undergrowth, swerving to avoid colliding with trees. Alfred held on to Saga. They pressed themselves down into the bear's fur to stay clear of the branches.

When Alfred glanced back, he saw three antlered wolves chasing after them from the perimeter of the forest. The pursuers were so close the cloud of bats couldn't hide them any longer.

The howls grew louder. Alfred peeked over his shoulder again. Now, there were five wolves. Two of them snapped at Bjørn's haunches.

Bjørn kicked at their antlers and hit one of them. It flew backwards with a high whine. The other fell back to the pack.

The next time Alfred looked, seven wolves pursued them, spread out in a half circle. The two frontrunners raced on either side of Bjørn, on the way to overtaking him. Soon they would be surrounded.

Bjørn grunted.

'Hold on!' Alfred yelled to Saga.

The powerful muscles under them tensed. Bjørn's hind legs pushed off. He jumped towards an opening in the ground. Weightless, Saga and Alfred hovered over the enormous bear, before they all started falling. Falling into a sinkhole.

With the two of them on his back, Bjørn slammed down onto the ground. His legs buckled, and his forepaws sank into the moss. Alfred banged his head against Saga's shoulder. Above, the pack howled.

While the bear got up on his paws, Saga and Alfred watched the ring of antlers. None of the wolves followed them, but their howls would alert the guards and high faeries.

The sinkhole was deep, but much smaller than the one they had climbed into earlier.

Bjørn grunted again. He sprang directly at one of the vine-covered walls. Alfred braced himself for the impact, but they flew straight through the plants and landed in a tunnel on top of Bjørn's embroidered shaggy coat. He was back in his almost-human shape.

'Okay, darlings?' he panted. 'That was close.'

Saga and Alfred climbed down from his back, and he eased himself up to sitting.

'Hurry. We're not in your realm yet. Follow Batty out.' Bjørn pointed at the bat that hung face down above them. 'I'll stay and guard the tunnel.'

Alfred supported Saga as they shuffled after the bat. She flew ahead of them in a tunnel lit up by glow worms until they reached the enormous dripstone cavern. The one without spirit prisons.

No light fell in through the cracks in the ceiling. Few worms glowed far above. In near darkness, they walked between the huge stalagmite columns.

Alfred wished he could see them one more time, see if they really were as impressive as he remembered. But it was too gloomy.

After Batty led them to a small hole in the wall at the lowest part of the cavern, she said, 'I'll be waiting here,' in an almost inaudible squeak.

On hands and knees, Alfred and Saga crawled through the hole into a narrow dusty burrow. Somewhere in the middle of the passage, the dust became dense grey haze. Although the children couldn't see anything, they crawled on. The grey haze clung to them until its particles evaporated.

They surfaced at the edge of the woods. Only one waning moon shone in the night sky. In the distance, the motorway's headlights and red stripes snaked through the dark landscape. The air was pleasant and fresh, with none of the fustiness of the air in the faerie realm.

'How long...' Alfred didn't finish his question.

Saga wiped her glasses on the inside of her T-shirt. 'It's silent. That's a good sign. No search parties.'

39

The Living Cottage

Without speaking, Saga and Alfred hobbled down past the tunnel building site and its strange mounds of creepers.

As they untangled their bicycles from the scrubs, Saga asked quietly, 'Do you think we can convince them?'

Alfred was surprised to hear his friend's doubt, but then noticed how weary and lost she looked. Saga might not be a faerie shapeshifter, but she had the heart of a lion and the wisdom of an owl.

'You're the bravest and smartest person I know, and your plan is brilliant,' he said, squashing his own worries.

It brought a smile to her smudged face.

They freewheeled down the track and along the road, the current of air tugging at Alfred's long curls. He'd lost the hairband in the river, and he didn't care. He just wanted to get home to Granny and call Dad. They were his family. They had always been his family.

'Isn't that your dad's car?' Saga asked as they approached Granny's cottage.

Alfred slowed and got off his bike by the rental car. Saga stopped too.

Beyond the gate, the garden was silent and the cottage dark.

'That's not a good sign,' Saga said. 'Is your phone still dead?'

When Alfred nodded, she said, 'Go inside and charge it. We need to know if it's still today. And bring me a small kitchen knife.'

Alfred hurried to the cottage. It seemed totally abandoned. A scrawled note hung on the door handle, saying that Granny and Dad were at Saga's house and to call Dad immediately. After unlocking the door, he hurried into his room and connected his phone to the charger. It was 10.37 p.m., but at least it was still the same date as when they'd left.

Without calling Dad, he fetched a small knife from the kitchen and jogged back to Saga to tell her what he'd discovered.

'Okay,' she said. 'Give me a five-minute head start. I need to stop and puncture my tyre before I get home.' She held her hand out for the knife. 'That's our story. We were on the other side of the Faerie Hill when it happened. We took a shortcut through the forest. That's where I twisted my ankle and we made our discovery.'

Back inside the cottage, after Saga had left, Alfred checked all the window sills. The woodcarvings stood in their usual spots. But they were as lifeless as any old carved pieces of wood.

In the hallway, he climbed up to replace the piece of kindling above the door with the fork-tongued spy.

The instant he set the horrible figurine down, a pulse, like an electric shock, sparkled between his fingers. He yanked his hand back. All the windows rattled. As if he'd restarted the heart of the cottage, it came alive with an energy that coursed through the other five carvings.

Afterwards, he called Dad from Granny's landline.

'We're on our way,' Dad said and hung up, before Alfred had a chance to speak. Saga must already be home.

In a frantic hurry, he washed his face and dirty hands and changed his clothes. One trouser leg was torn to shreds, from when Bjørn had freed him from the living prison bars. His T-shirt had a large hole on the back, and he doubted it would ever become clean again. But he was ready by the time Granny and Dad rushed into the cottage.

'Oh, thank goodness,' Granny said and enveloped him in her arms.

Dad hugged him too—a fierce, never-letting-go hug that squeezed all the air out of Alfred.

After Granny muttered something about putting the kettle on, she closed the kitchen door behind her.

Dad's hug was so tight Alfred could feel him shaking. Abruptly, he let go and pushed Alfred away, down onto the stool. Standing over him, Dad started shouting like never before. Alfred didn't even try to defend himself. He knew why Dad had been worried sick, and at every accusation of his own thoughtlessness, he just said he was sorry. And he meant it. Soon, Dad crouched and hugged him again.

'You can't worry Granny like that, Alfie.' Dad ruffled his long hair with a puzzled look. 'I'm sorry I didn't have time to come here sooner.'

It seemed like it was ages ago he'd called Dad, wanting to ask if he was Dad's real son.

Of course he was. It didn't matter whether Dad was his biological father. Dad had always taken care of him. He'd always be there when Alfred needed him. Dad loved him, and he loved Dad. They belonged together, no matter what he discovered about his faerie parents.

'...So we're all set for tomorrow. I have an overview of all the geological data. Unfortunately, the most recent dataset was wrong. It was from one of the guys who was recovered from the sinkhole. His equipment must've been damaged.'

'No! You can't drill into the Faerie Hill, Dad. We've found something...'

Sitting in the kitchen with Granny, drinking tea and devouring a plateful of blueberry muffins, Alfred explained. Between mouthfuls, he told them what he and Saga had agreed, omitting any mention of faeries or shapeshifters or their visit to another realm.

While he talked, he tried not to look at Granny. Whenever he met her blue eyes, he could see that she knew there was more to the story. Behind her, the bat's ears twitched.

'So, you see, Dad, we need time to convince the mayor before the mole arrives and starts drilling.'

Dad was frowning, muttering, 'But the geological data doesn't show—'

'What about that dataset you mentioned? What if it isn't wrong?'

'I suppose...' Dad narrowed his eyes and looked sideways, while he thought. 'I suppose that could indicate that something's there.'

'I'm telling you, it's there. Trust me!'

Dad nodded as he got up. 'Alright,' he said. 'I need to make some calls and get hold of the outlier dataset. I'll pick you up before seven, and then you'll show me—'

'The most spectacular dripstone cavern you've ever seen,' Alfred said, hoping very much it was true.

40

Under the Wood

After Granny had gone to bed, Alfred sneaked into the kitchen and talked to Saga on the phone until past midnight. So far, everyone had agreed to come. Still, everything depended on how those people would react. If Saga was right, they might stop the tunnel project and save the pond and the Faerie Hill. And then he would finally learn the truth about himself. But what if Batty was right, and the cavern was nothing special?

He'd lain awake until three o'clock in the morning, staring up at the river tapestry, missing the little water-sprite figurine and wondering what the day would bring.

At dawn, he stood in the kitchen, drinking tea, while he looked out beyond the carved bear. Dew glittered on the lawn. A tint of orange coloured the pale morning sky. A hedgehog—a real hedgehog—snuffled along the brambles. When the garden gate slammed shut after Dad, it vanished under the hedgerow.

Dad ran up the path, waving a wad of paper, with a huge smile on his face. Alfred flung the front door open.

'It fits, Alfie! The geo data fits.' He grabbed Alfred with one arm and swung him around as if he were still a toddler.

Granny chuckled all the way to the car where she ushered Alfred into the passenger seat and climbed in behind him.

'I can't tell you how relieved I am,' Dad said, as they were driving up the lane. Alfred glanced sideways at him, wondering if deep down Dad had been hoping for something like this to happen all along.

They arrived at the track up to the building site at the same time as Saga. She waved from her uncle's green minivan. Halfway up the dirt road, two tractors blocked the cars. Saga's dad jumped down from one and greeted them. Together, they all continued on foot. Saga's ankle had been properly bandaged, and she'd brought a trekking pole as support.

'What about the vines? We have to stop anyone from touching them,' Alfred hissed, dragging Saga along, overtaking the others. He'd completely forgotten to tell Dad about the overgrown machinery. 'And how do we explain them?'

A car honked behind them. Two black cars had arrived by the tractors. The mayor stepped out from the backseat of one. The woman from the planning commission emerged from the other. Waving his arms and shouting something, the mayor stomped up towards them, with the woman and their assistants in his wake. With everyone distracted by the new arrivals, Saga and Alfred hurried ahead of the rest of their group.

Granny would know the plants came from the faerie realm. Perhaps she could help weave a tale to explain their presence.

Alfred needn't have worried. The vines were gone. Or almost gone.

Whoever controlled the poisonous faerie plants apparently believed in their plan.

The gravel plane lay bare. The plants had released the shipping container offices and most of the heavy machinery. Only the three yellow diggers by the cliff were still partly entangled in creepers.

Intrigued, the group headed there, ignoring Saga's suggestion that they go directly to the cavern.

'Don't touch them!' Alfred called out, as her uncle knelt to inspect one of the purple-veined leaves.

'I've never seen anything like it,' Saga's uncle said, leaning closer and prodding the vine with a ballpoint pen. 'Must be some invasive plant from abroad. Do you know what it is, Rob?'

'Some sort of poison ivy?' Dad said. 'What do you think, Mum?'

Granny glanced at Alfred. Before she could answer, the mayor and his staff caught up.

'What's all this? Applevale, are you in cahoots with those... those tree huggers?' The mayor wrinkled his nose, exposing yellow teeth below his moustache.

'Saga here discovered the cavern together with my son,' Dad said.

'I don't know what you think you're playing at.' The mayor waved his arm at Saga's uncle. 'This is private property. You have no right to be here. And those plant thingies... That's sabotage. Applevale, find someone to get rid of these people. I want my tunnel!'

'Why don't we all take a look at the cavern? If it is as magnificent as my son tells me...' Dad held up his report with the geo data. 'And based on the most recent data, I believe it might be.'

'Pah! Who cares about dripstones?' The mayor huffed.

Surprising himself, Alfred decided to speak up. 'Saga says the cavern is much bigger than the other caves around here. It's at least 250 metres long and probably half as wide.'

The mayor raised a bushy eyebrow, asking, '250 metres? Really?'

Saga nodded.

The mayor stared at her for a second, then looked back to Alfred. 'Let's see it then, young man.'

'Lead the way, young man and young woman,' Saga's uncle said in a good imitation of the mayor's pompous voice.

With a line of people behind them, Saga and Alfred walked up towards the edge of the forest. The mayor complained about ruining his shoes.

'Can you walk faster?' Alfred asked. The sun had risen above the trees, and his shadow had appeared. Saga's, of course, had not.

'I wouldn't mind if I don't get my shadow back,' she said quietly. 'Maybe I'm the only shadowless person in the whole world. That'd be quite extraordinary.'

Alfred shook his head. He really didn't understand her wish to stand out.

Outside the entrance, they paused to admire the work Marjorie and her mole friends had done during the night. The previous evening, they had crawled through a narrow passage. Now, Alfred and Saga could walk upright into the cavern. There was no grey haze.

Inside, they waited for everyone to enter. Dad had brought torches, but sunlight sliced through the gaps in the ceiling, illuminating the dripstones. The sight was even more spectacular than Alfred recalled.

One by one, the rest of the group stepped in through the

opening. Upon entering, they all reacted with stunned silence, followed by awed whispers. All but the mayor.

He stood with crossed arms and muttered something about his tunnel.

'This is longer than 250 metres,' Dad said, his eyes gleaming.

The mayor's bushy eyebrows furrowed.

'Perhaps you could name it Underwood Cavern?' Alfred suggested. It seemed rather fitting.

Saga pinched him and grinned.

'Underwood Cavern...' the mayor repeated, letting his arms fall and his forehead relax. 'Not a bad idea, young man. Not a bad idea at all.'

While everyone was admiring the breathtaking formations, Alfred walked all the way up through the cavern. He thought he remembered where the tunnel used to be, but it was already so well hidden he couldn't find the exact spot.

His hand hovered in front of a particularly smooth section of the wall. Had Marjorie and her team of moles moved both the physical barrier and the veil of grey haze? Or was this border shut, with no passable mist between the worlds?

That the realms might be this close together seemed strange. And strangely ominous.

Without touching the wall, he returned to the group.

The mayor had completely changed his tune. He was speaking with Granny and Saga's uncle, saying how much more impressive the cavern was than those in the neighbouring county. And he asked about the likelihood of obtaining Natural World Heritage Site status for Underwood Cavern.

Saga's uncle said sightings of rare bats in the area would benefit their application.

The woman from the regional planning commission kept muttering something about wasted man-hours and budgets and how many phone calls she would have to make.

Above her, a bat let go of its hold on the ceiling and flew out of the cavern.

Dad stood, looking around the enormous space, smiling in a way that Alfred thought of as his sad smile. He knew it had nothing to do with him losing this job and everything to do with Nereida.

It was only now Alfred realized that without the tunnel project job, Dad would need to accept one of the other offers he'd received. Before their furniture had even arrived, they would move again. And, for the first time in his life, Alfred didn't want to move away.

Saga was the best friend he'd ever had. He enjoyed spending time with Granny. And there was Batty and Bjørn and the other creatures... He wouldn't even mind hanging out with Mr Tumbleweed.

There was also something else he couldn't explain that bound him here. Roots deep inside him connected him to the land, to the Faerie Hill, and most of all to its rivers and streams.

Dad left the others and sidled up to him. He reached up to tousle Alfred's long hair, frowning, as if inwardly calculating how many days had passed since the last haircut.

'You like it here, don't you, Alfie?'

Alfred nodded.

'I'd better look for a job that's not too far away, then, so we can visit often.'

Alfred threw his arms round his dad, mumbling, 'That would be great, Dad,' into his shoulder

'That would indeed be great,' Granny said, right next to them.

'Applevale!' the mayor called. 'We're off to my office to tie up all the loose ends and register the name of the cavern.'

'It's okay.' Alfred let go of Dad. 'I'm going with Saga to the pond,' he said, and gave Granny a hug.

In the confusion of everyone leaving, Saga and Alfred slipped away, heading not to the pond but into the woods to find the shapeshifters.

41

Faerie Blood

They had not walked far when Bjørn found them.

'I knew you could do it!' He enveloped them in a furry bear hug, squashing Alfred's nose against an embroidered bee. 'Evie is on the way with your shadow, darling,' he said to Saga.

Alfred's mind formed an image of a shadow hurtling through the air, landing at Saga's feet and snapping itself onto her like it was magnetic. It made him smile. But, of course, he knew Evie the eagle would bring the shadow, and attaching it surely wouldn't be that easy.

'You look exactly like your dad when you smile,' Saga said.

'Do I?'

'You do.' Bjørn nodded sagely. 'It's the Applevale smile.'

'And like you, he doesn't talk much, does he? Mum says he was always the quiet sort.'

Alfred supposed it was normal that he was a bit like Dad, who'd raised him. 'Do you always say everything that's on your mind?'

'Pretty much.' Saga giggled.

Alfred snorted and Bjørn's chuckles rumbled.

In high spirits, with the shapeshifter's enormous hands clasped round their shoulders, they walked off the path, behind a rocky outcrop and in among the densest trees. Further away in the undergrowth, a rushing sound came from the vines that were flowing back towards the sinkhole.

'We're almost at the meeting point,' Bjørn said. 'Make sure you show Evie respect. She appreciates that.'

A short while later, the trees opened into a circular clearing. On a boulder in its centre sat a white-haired woman in a long dress the exact same warm shade of brown as her skin tone. She had a beaky nose and the most piercing eyes Alfred had ever seen. Yellow eyes.

The woman reminded him of a school librarian, on the watch for food and folded page corners. It made him immediately trust her, because librarians were kind and helpful and always ready to provide sanctuary from bullies. Wiggling from her claw-like hands were two rat-sized pixies.

Alfred greeted her by saying, in a loud voice, 'Hello, Miss Evie.'

'I am not deaf, young sprite. And I am not a "miss",' she said, enunciating each word. 'Look what I have brought for your friend. Come here, human girl. Sit.' She pointed at the nearest boulder, using one of the pixies. Little Mother. Upside down, her layers of smudged petticoats made her resemble a strange grey flower with her clogs as pollen on chubby stamens.

Saga shuffled forward. Evie let the little people down. They trudged to Saga's feet, while Evie placed a semi-transparent roll on the ground.

'Put her feet together, Little Father, so I only have to do one seam.' Little Mother said in her screechy voice, wielding a silver needle as long as her arm.

'You will do no such thing,' Evie said. 'Or her shadow will crinkle at the bottom.'

Little Father muttered, 'At least she wore the same boots.' He tugged at Saga's bootlaces, directing her feet until they were exactly as far apart as they'd been when her shadow was stolen.

Bjørn took off his hairy coat. Underneath he was wearing a just-as-hairy jumper. After sinking down on the ground, he pulled needles and colourful threads out of a coat pocket. He repaired the bee on the shoulder, while he kept glancing at what Little Mother was doing.

'Such a pretty shadow,' Little Mother said. 'Isn't it, Little Father?' She made the first stitch with the long silver needle and midnight-black gossamer. 'Can you spare a snippet for a kind soul?'

'Don't listen to her, darling,' Bjørn said. 'She was never a kind soul.'

Little Father rolled the shadow out flat on the ground.

For two whole stitches, Little Mother sewed in silence. Every stitch took minutes, because it was a full body exercise for the pixie. She had to take ten steps to pull the thread through, and ten steps back to Saga. Here, she plunged the needle into a spot that was just between the soles of Saga's hiking boots and the surrounding air. A spot only Little Mother could see, Evie explained. All of this had to be done carefully to avoid the gossamer thread from breaking.

'Only a lazy tailor sews with a long thread,' Bjørn muttered.

'Human girl... Er... Darling, don't you think we are doing a nice job? Wouldn't you want Little Father and myself to get a small payment for our hard work?' asked Little Mother.

'Work you would not have to do, had you not stolen her shadow,' Evie commented.

'Alright.' Saga made a fist with her little finger sticking out. 'You can have the shadow of my left little finger if you promise never to harm me or Nemo or steal shadows from any other human ever again.'

'That's a steep price, Little Mother,' said Little Father, like a seasoned haggler. 'Shadows fetch a good price in shady deals.'

'I know, and I do like the snip, snip, snip of the silver scissors... But I can see that little finger as our bedchamber curtain. If I stretch it a bit...'

'Are you sure?' Alfred asked Saga. 'Someone might notice.'

She shrugged. 'So what? I don't mind.'

Little Mother stuck the silver needle into the rubber sole of Saga's hiking boots and scuttled over to the left hand of the still shadow with her silver scissors. Saga wiggled her little finger, but the shadow didn't move.

'Not like that.' One of Evie's claw-like hands shot down and turned Little Mother and her scissors, so she was pointing across the finger below the joint. The pixie had been about to cut from the gap between the little finger and the ring finger down towards the wrist.

'But the bones below belong to the little finger,' Little Mother protested, before she hurried to cut across the dark shadow.

Little Father clapped his round stomach. 'Little Mother never promised not to snip animals and shapeshifters and other creatures,' he said and giggled hysterically.

'Back to work.' Evie grabbed the pixie and pinched the little-finger shadow, saying the little people would only get it if Saga's shadow was perfect after the operation.

Grumbling, Little Mother continued to sew. She wasn't even halfway on the first foot and Alfred was getting impatient.

'Will you tell me about my parents now?' he asked Bjørn.

'Wouldn't you rather wait till nightfall and hear everything from Batty?'

But Alfred couldn't wait any longer. 'They are water sprites, right?'

'Let's just get away from prying ears.' Bjørn heaved himself up from the ground. 'I don't mean you, darling,' he said to Saga, and led Alfred to the edge of the clearing. 'Of course, your mother's a water sprite. How could she be anything else? How could you be anything else? The way you swim... Batty and I saw you fight in the river.'

Alfred drew a deep breath, relieved to get this question answered. 'Where is she?'

'Oh, honey, I wish I knew. I miss her terribly.' Bjørn stared into empty space. 'She was always the kindest of the faeries. I'm not speaking in past tense because I think she is dead, only because everything happened long ago. Once, when I was a cub, I fell in the river, because that other one... The mean one...'

'Lillith?'

'Yes, Lillith. Her slimy strands tripped me. On purpose, I'm sure. But your mother caught me, and she helped me learn to swim, cradling me in her hair, even though I was just a shapeshifter. Lillith mocked her for helping lost creatures like me, or Evie when she'd broken a wing, or Castor when a waterfall threw him up on dry land.'

'Is he the catfish?'

Bjørn nodded. 'Castor always thought Lillith had slung him out of the water, just to get rid of one of your mother's friends. She was so jealous of your mother. And now she swims in all her old streams as if she owns them.'

The more Alfred heard about his faerie mother, the more he wished to find her.

The more he heard about Lillith, the less he liked her.

'I got the feeling Lillith disliked me,' Alfred said, although dislike was a very mild word for the hatred that had shone out of her green orb-like eyes.

'I'm sure she does. First of all, you look so much like your mother—anyone can see that. Secondly, I don't think she likes mix-bloods like us. And I'm not trying to compare myself to you. I'm only a shapeshifter. Although you're half human, you have water-sprite blood and abilities.'

'Why does that make a difference?'

'Those with powers of enchantment have always ruled our realm. And water sprites are almost as powerful as the high faeries.'

Alfred thought about the creatures he'd seen, from the butterfly faeries and necklace beetles to the antlered wolves. They all served the high faeries. Then he realized what Bjørn had said.

'I'm half human? So I'm not a changeling? My faerie blood... It's because my dad and this water sprite—'

'A changeling? How could you get such an absurd idea? Wait till I tell Batty!' Bjørn chuckled. 'The greatest love story in our part of the realm is the tale of Nereida and Applevale. The fish in her old streams still sing the song about all she went through for her love of a human.'

Like water dripping from Granny's wet yarn, the puzzle pieces fell into place. Everyone had said he looked like Nereida, but no one had mentioned Nereida wasn't human. When

Lillith said his mother had gone into another realm, she hadn't meant into Faerie but out into the human world.

He had his faerie blood from Nereida, and his human blood from his father.

'But how could everyone see Nereida if she's a faerie?' he asked, recalling Saga's rejection of this idea.

'Oh, the only reason they can't see us is because we hide behind glamour. I could show myself to all humans if I wanted to.' Bjørn beamed, displaying his sharp fangs. 'They'd probably run away screaming...'

A glow spread from Alfred's heart. Nereida was a water sprite, and she was his mother! He still didn't know why she had left twelve years ago or what had happened to her, but it was a start. The water-sprite figurine must be portraying her. From the first time he saw it, he'd loved the woodcarving and sensed a connection.

Bjørn was still chuckling and muttering, 'a changeling,' when another squabble broke out with the little people. 'I'd better help Evie,' he said, and lumbered back to the group.

Alfred stayed by the edge of the clearing, thinking and listening to the tinkling music of a nearby stream. He was so absorbed, it took a while before he noticed something was fluttering right in front of his face.

It was a blue butterfly faerie, and it was waving its tiny arms for him to follow.

'I'll be right back,' he called to the group around Saga, as he stepped after the flittering creature.

42

A Tempting Offer

Amanita was waiting for him by a cluster of pines. Alfred saw her as soon as he left the clearing. He knew what she wanted.

'I don't need you to tell me about my parents, and I already have protection,' he called. 'So I'm not giving you the figurine.'

In the silence that followed this outburst, the butterfly faerie fluttered back to its position in Amanita's hair.

Alfred halted a few metres from the pines. 'And we stopped the tunnel project,' he added.

'By giving them access to part of our realm.' She shook her head. The butterfly faeries scrambled to hold on. 'I suppose it could have been worse. But will one cavern satisfy them? Humans are always greedy when it comes to nature. They believe they can take without giving back.'

With gliding strides, Amanita came so close to him he could feel the cool musty air wafting off her mossy dress.

'Your mother was wise when she chose your name.'

'Nemo?' Alfred asked hesitantly.

'We both know that is not your name, Alfred.' Amanita smiled. 'Do you know what it means?'

He shook his head.

'Alf rät,' she said. 'Elvish council. An advisor to elves and faeries. And you have already had your first success, stopping the humans from drilling desolation into our realm.'

'That wasn't me. Saga had the ideas. And Ba—' He caught himself from using their names. 'And the shapeshifters did all the work.'

'Every leader needs a good supporting team.'

'They weren't supporting me! I'm not the leader.'

Amanita ignored him, saying, 'In the realm, you would have an even better team than that raggedy band of creatures. There are others like you, you know. Gifted demi-fae with human blood. They would welcome you.'

Others like him. Human-faeries? Faerie-humans? Alfred's mind began spinning, wondering how it would feel to not be an outsider.

As if she read his mind, Amanita said, 'Your queen wants you to join their ranks. We are your family. You belong to us.'

He imagined that instead of going to a normal school, he would set out for the faerie realm every morning. Without asking, he knew that wasn't what Amanita or the queen had in mind.

'What about my dad and grandmother?'

'Oh, that is not a problem. We shall make them forget. Whenever they think about you, they will remember a boy they loved long ago. They will feel a sadness so deep their fragile human brains will shy away from the painful memory, lest it scatters them. A breath later, their minds will skip to a less unpleasant thought.'

Alfred's breath caught. He recognized precisely what she was describing.

'That's what happens when they think about my mother,' he whispered past a lump that constricted his throat.

Amanita's eyebrows shot up in surprise.

Even in his sadness, he could've kicked himself for revealing something she clearly hadn't known. However, now that he had told her, he asked, 'Can you make them remember?'

Amanita shook her head. 'Nereida must have made them forget. Impressive!' She smiled again. 'Only she would be able to remove the enchantment she has woven.'

Why had his mother made those who loved her forget? Had she simply wanted them to forget she wasn't human? Then, when she disappeared, had something gone wrong so they forgot almost everything about her? Could that be the explanation?

He didn't ask. Amanita wouldn't know. Only his mother knew the answer. Like a kernel of resin, smaller even than the tiny resin tear on the figurine of the water sprite—of her—Alfred saved the question deep in his core. He hoped that one day, magically, like when resin turned into amber, everything would become transparent, revealing the answer.

'I can't leave Dad and Granny.'

'There is no need to decide now. The queen's offer stands. You will still be welcomed in a few years when they are gone.'

Alfred gasped. 'Gone? In a few years? What do you mean?'

'You still think in human time spans. How endearing.' Amanita giggled. Even the butterfly faeries tittered. 'Soon you are fully grown and stop ageing, and then you will find it difficult to stay with them, constantly seeing the reflection of their confusion. Blink twice, and all the humans you know will be in their graves.'

There hadn't been a birthday on his mother's grave. For all he knew, she could've been a thousand years old. Would he live for centuries, while everyone around him grew old and died?

'I can see what you fear,' Amanita said. 'Come with me, and you will not have to suffer.'

Alfred's mind raced. If he accepted the faerie queen's offer, he would be among like-minded creatures. With the queen behind him, he wouldn't be afraid of Lillith. He would be able to hear the song the fish sang about Nereida's love for a human. He could get hold of the water-sprite figurine. And perhaps, if it was like the spirit prisons in the cave, the queen could free his mother. If not, he might still find her. If she existed anywhere, it would be in the faerie realm.

It was so, so tempting.

But then Alfred thought about Dad and Granny and Saga, who had become the best friend he'd always wanted. And he knew he couldn't leave them, no matter how much it would hurt later.

'You belong with us.' Amanita held out her hand. Her bracelet snake slithered around her wrist.

Where did he belong?

He envied Lillith, who so clearly belonged in her rivers and streams with their connections between the realms. If he couldn't have both worlds, it felt like he would never belong in either. But he would have to make a choice and live with it for a long time.

In so many ways, he was like his mother, and she had literally been a fish out of water among humans. In other ways, though, he resembled Dad. He could see that now. Not just their mannerisms, but they had lots of other little things—human things—in common. And Alfred couldn't imagine a life without his father.

Perhaps knowing why he was different would make him worry less about fitting in. Perhaps he could even follow

Saga's example and revel in standing out—or at least try not to hide so much.

Maybe what really mattered, he realized, was simply how he lived his life: choosing to belong somewhere, without giving up any part of himself.

'Come.'

'Not yet.' Alfred turned away from Amanita, saying, 'I belong here.'

'For now,' she replied.

All the way back to the clearing, he felt the stare of her bottomless black eyes.

 43

The Return of the Water Sprite

Bjørn carried the children to the edge of the forest close to Granny's cottage. While they limped down through the meadow, Alfred recounted to Saga everything Bjørn had told him and part of what Amanita had said. A small part. Mainly, that he was both human and faerie, and that there were others like him. He didn't mention his prospects of an abnormally long life.

Saga nodded and smiled knowingly, as if nothing surprised her.

When they stopped by Granny's hedgerow, she said, 'You wanna see something cool?' With her back to the sun, she raised both arms above her head, spread her fingers wide and wiggled them a bit.

Alfred gazed at her shadow, from her feet past the mouse-ear buns to her left hand with its four fingers. He couldn't help chuckling.

'I know when we first met I said it was a pity we couldn't be friends, because the tunnel project would be cancelled and you'd move away,' she said. 'Now, I'm almost sad we stopped it so soon, because we are friends now, right? Even if Mr Tumbleweed comes back, you're my best friend.'

'Of course.' Alfred cleared his throat. No one had ever called him their best friend. 'You're my best friend too. Even if Mr Tumbleweed comes back.'

They both burst out laughing.

'And, after I move away, we can still chat online...' he said, although that seemed rather tame compared to what they had been doing the last days.

'Oh, definitely. There's so much to do. I'm going to make a plan.'

'A plan?' What was she up to now?

'Yeah. A plan for the work of the Faerie Investigation Society. You're a founding member, so I expect you to help. First, we have to compile everything we've learnt about the faeries. We'll start tomorrow...'

Saga talked on. Alfred just agreed to everything. Although it sounded a bit like a school project, he was looking forward to the work. Having a best friend made all the difference. Saga might be a little odd, but he liked that about her and he trusted her completely. Tomorrow, he'd tell her all the details he'd withheld from his talk with Amanita.

Their Faerie Investigation Society work also meant they would stay in touch, no matter where he and dad moved next, and she could keep him up to date on what was happening in the woods.

It would help prepare him for his return to Faerie. Because he would be going back, and not to fulfil whatever plan Amanita and the queen had for his long life. Some day soon, Alfred would return, and he hoped Saga would come with him.

He couldn't wait until he was a grown-up to find out what had happened to his mother or listen to the song the fish sang about her and Dad—the tale of Nereida and Applevale. And Alfred wished they could help the Duke of Burgundy. The possibility of meeting the faerie queen gave him the chills, but when he thought about the tiny heartbroken faerie, he knew they had to find a way to free all the captured spirits.

More pressing than anything else was his wish to rescue the water-sprite figurine. He yearned to hold her. She belonged with him. There must be a way to reclaim her from Lillith.

'This one body is right here, and some bodies don't even notice,' a familiar creaking-floorboard voice grumbled.

'Mr Tumbleweed! You're back!' Saga swung the strange creature up and clutched him to her chest. Alfred patted the tree sprite's lichen-covered arm.

'The other somebodies are even not nicer than these somebodies, and this one body prefers the cakes here!'

'Then let's go home and bake a cake. Are you coming, Alfred?'

'Perhaps later,' he replied and opened Granny's gate.

As he stepped from stone to stone on the garden path, he looked up at the cliff behind the cottage. The sun lit up the steep rock wall. On its rim, the trees sighed in the breeze. The crows descended towards him. Their caws sounded friendly, like the barks of tail-wagging dogs, welcoming him home.

From above the front door, the fork-tongued figurine glared at him. He didn't attempt to hide from it by trying to turn invisible. Perhaps he would never want to be invisible again. Saga could see him and knew who and what he was, and she still liked him. Maybe others could learn to like him too, if he stopped hiding.

Alfred walked all the way round the cottage, stopping by each of the woodcarvings to place a fingertip on their windows. The slight vibrations in the glass made him feel warm inside. Warm and protected.

Granny had fallen asleep in a deckchair outside her shed. As quietly as possible, he slid the bolts aside and entered the cave. Before turning on the light, he stood for a moment, watching the turquoise ribbon of water disappear into the darkness.

After flipping the switch, he grabbed a big torch, which Granny kept in the shed in case there was a power outage, and ducked under the bundles of hanging yarn.

Here, the walls curved in and the ceiling down, until the cave became a tunnel. The music from the spring sounded louder and echoed in the narrow space.

He didn't walk far before the stream filled the whole width of the tunnel. The ground and walls made a perfectly smooth pipe, formed by millennia of meltwater. He crouched on the last bit of dry surface and cast the light of the torch into the black hole. It was a connection to the river—traces of its song rang clear and true in the stream, and his shoes had floated here.

A movement caught his attention. Snagged by a ragged rock, bobbing in the water, was a snippet of turquoise yarn. The snippet Saga had thrown into the underground crevice.

Would the channel be big enough for him to swim through? If so, it might take him all the way to Faerie.

Every part of him longed to be reunited with the clear water. But the streams belonged to Lillith.

Here goes nothing, Alfred thought. Still wearing his shoes, he stepped into the water. It swirled around his ankles and rose to fill the tunnel. After lying down on his elbows and stomach, his head became submerged. He blinked a few times until his eyes could stay open in the rush.

The stream's music and the song of the fish filled his ears. His hair danced like fluttering streamers on a windy day. It was wonderful.

Alfred opened his mouth, letting the stream flow through him. He could taste all the different turquoise colours. The trickle by his ears increased.

'Lillith!' he called as loud as he could.

The song of the fish stilled.

'Lillith. I want the water-sprite figurine back. I know it's my mother, and I want it.' His words matched the rhythm of the current.

The fish chorused, '*Lil-lil-lillith...*'

Alfred was certain she could hear him. But she didn't answer.

He'd learnt how much faeries liked to make deals, but he couldn't trade any of the other carvings for the figurine. There was, however, one thing he knew she wanted. Or rather, didn't want.

His mother had been her rival, that much was clear. Perhaps she saw him as a rival too, or she wouldn't have looked at him with such hatred.

'Lillith, if you give me the figurine...' he began, then thought better of it, because he couldn't promise that he wouldn't ever come back. 'If you don't give me the figurine, I'll return to the faerie realm every single day and swim in your river.'

'*In the depth of the stream-stream-stream,*' the fish sang, '*Nereida's son proposed a deal-deal-deal. And Lil-lil-Lillith—*'

'Leave my stream,' Lillith sang. Her clear soprano voice drowned out the choir. A fist-sized bundle of her hair came into view. It unfurled in front of Alfred, releasing the figurine.

The moment it was freed, Alfred grasped the little water sprite. Clutching her in his hand, he let the current carry him out of the tunnel and into the shallow spring. Here, he crawled up on the dry stone floor and past the curtain of hanging yarn.

In the harsh light inside the cave, he sat down between the dye baths and stroked the long hair of the figurine. Immediately, he felt a deep sense of relief. His own wet hair hung down past his shoulders, dripping on the water sprite. His clothes were drenched, but a glowing warmth spread in his whole body.

'Mother,' he whispered. 'Mum. Can you hear me?'

He caressed her cheek, meaning to brush at the tiny resin tear. It wasn't there.

Something else was different too. Had Lillith tricked him? Was this a different figurine?

He brought the water sprite up to eye level, turning it, studying all the minute details. It was definitely the same figurine, although the tear was gone, and her expression had changed. She didn't look sad and wistful any more. She was smiling—a satisfied, knowing smile.

He had found her, and she knew it.

Alfred smiled back at her, a tear rolling down his cheek. He didn't bother wiping it away.

'Mum,' he whispered again.

Without a shadow of doubt, he knew the water-sprite figurine sheltered his mother's spirit.

ACKNOWLEDGEMENTS

My first thanks go to all the trees in the forest behind our house. During several pandemic lockdowns, they let me walk among them and imagine strange creatures peeping out of their shadows. I stepped into faerie rings, which may or may not have taken me to another realm. At times, it certainly felt as if time stood still.

Other forests and underground caves on four continents have inspired the setting of this story too—from my childhood forests in Denmark all the way to the underground river in the Waitomo Glowworm caves in New Zealand and dripstone caverns in Vietnam. I'm thankful that I have had the opportunity to travel and explore so many breathtaking places that feed my imagination.

I wouldn't have been able to write without close friends and family, so huge thanks to my loved ones, especially to Claus, August and Marcus for giving me space to write when we were all cooped up together and for sometimes coming along on my forest walks. To my father for instilling in me a love of nature and the outdoors. To my mother-in-law for taking me to Mønsted Kalkgruber—the largest limestone mine in the world—on an exploration of its maze of tunnels, underground lakes and colonies of bats. And to my sister for early reading and on-demand cheerleading.

Without the help of an amazing group of talented people, my written words would never have become this finished book. I'm immensely grateful to Sarah Odedina for her help in shaping and finding the heart of this story and her enthusiasm for vicious faeries. To Tilda Johnson for showing me where clarity and improvements were needed—her eagle eyes are only surpassed by Evie's. To Thy Bui for the stunning cover and the gorgeous map of the Faerie Hill. To the whole wonderful team at Pushkin Press and the sales team at Bounce for producing a beautiful book and sending it out into the world.

During the last couple of years with limited in-person meetups, online connections have become even more important. And with my last book coming out during one of the lockdowns, the support of book bloggers, teachers, librarians, booksellers and other authors has been crucial and in many cases the lifeline that kept me hopeful and writing. I want to thank everyone who promotes books and reading on social media and in schools and bookshops, and I would like to mention some of the absolute stars who have gone above and beyond to support me. So, from the bottom of my heart, thanks to: Sinéad O'Hart, Juliette Forrest, Victoria Williamson, Piers Torday, Eloise Williams, Fleur Hitchcock, Pip Harry, Nadia King, Dominique Valente, Jo Cotterill, Jenni Spangler, Denise Tan, Dan Bassett, Liam James, Hayley W, Rina D, Rosie B, Chris Soul, KC, Gavin Hetherington, Nia Liversuch, Rich Simpson, Kate Heap, Karen Wall, Veronica Price, Jack Graves, Margaret Pemberton, Erin Hamilton, Naomi Cher, Rumena Aktar, Kevin Cobane, Valda Varadinek, Barbara V, Jacqui Sydney, Vicky Hassall, Emma Kuyateh, Catherine Friess, Scott Evans, Tamsin Rosewell, Rachael B, Nick Campbell and the Writers & Illustrators of Zurich.

Finally, huge thanks to all young activists who fight to protect nature, and to you, dear reader, for coming along on this adventure. If you ever see Bjørn in the woods, don't run away. He just wants to give you a bear hug.

MORE ADVENTURES BY H.S. NORUP